Snake on a Pole

The Hope of Righteousness by Faith

Brent Chrishon

TEACH Services, Inc.
PUBLISHING
www.TEACHServices.com • (800) 367-1844

The author assumes full responsibility for the accuracy of all facts and quotations as cited in this book. The opinions expressed in this book are the author's personal views and interpretations, and do not necessarily reflect those of the publisher.

This book is provided with the understanding that the publisher is not engaged in giving spiritual, legal, medical, or other professional advice. If authoritative advice is needed, the reader should seek the counsel of a competent professional.

ISBN-13: 978-1-4796-1504-9 (Paperback)

ISBN-13: 978-1-4796-1505-6 (ePub)

Library of Congress Control Number: 2022919533

All scripture quotations, unless otherwise indicated, are taken from the KING JAMES VERSION (KJV): KING JAMES VERSION, public domain.

Scripture quotations marked as (ARV) are taken from the American Revised Version. Scotland: Thomas Nelson & Sons, 1901.

Scriptures marked (ASV) are taken from the *New American Standard Bible*. La Habra, CA: Foundation Publications/Lockman Foundation, 1971.

Scriptures marked (BSB) are taken from The Holy Bible, Berean Study Bible (BSB), copyright © 2016 by Bible Hub. Used by Permission. All Rights Reserved Worldwide.

Scriptures marked (ESV) are taken from THE HOLY BIBLE, ENGLISH STANDARD VERSION (ESV): Scriptures taken from THE HOLY BIBLE, ENGLISH STANDARD VERSION ® Copyright© 2001 by Crossway, a publishing ministry of Good News Publishers. Used by permission.

Scriptures marked (GNB) are taken from the GOOD NEWS BIBLE (GNB): Scriptures taken from the Good News Bible, copyright © 1994, published by the Bible Societies/HarperCollins Publishers Ltd UK, Good News Bible © American Bible Society 1966, 1971, 1992. Used with permission.

Scriptures marked (NIV) are taken from the NEW INTERNATIONAL VERSION (NIV): Scripture taken from THE HOLY BIBLE, NEW INTERNATIONAL VERSION ®. Copyright© 1973, 1978, 1984, 2011 by Biblica, Inc.TM. Used by permission of Zondervan Bible Publishers.

Scriptures marked (NLT) are taken from the HOLY BIBLE, NEW LIVING TRANSLATION (NLT): Scriptures taken from the HOLY BIBLE, NEW LIVING TRANSLAION, Copyright© 1996, 2004, 2007, by Tyndale House Foundation. Used by permission of Tyndale HousePublishers, Inc., Carol Stream, Illinois 60188. All rights reserved. Used by permission.

Scriptures marked (NRSV) are taken from the New Revised Standard Version Bible, copyright © 1989. National Council of the Churches of Christ in the United States of America. Used by permission. All rights reserved worldwide.

Scriptures are also taken from Murdock, James. *Murdock's Translation of the Aramaic New Testament*, 1852.

TEACH Services, Inc.

P U B L I S H I N G

www.TEACHServices.com • (800) 367-1844

This work is dedicated to the Testator of the Covenant: Jesus Christ and His bride: the Israel of God.

"O Yahuwah, I have heard thy speech, and was afraid: O Yahuwah, revive thy work in the midst of the years, in the midst of the years make known; in wrath remember mercy."
Habakkuk 3:2

CONTENTS

I

Thou shalt have no other gods before Me

II

You shalt not make unto thee any graven image,or any likeness of anything that is in Haven above,or that is in the earth beneth,or that is in the water under the earth : thou shalt not bow down thyself to them nor serv them: For I the lord thy God am a jealous God visiting the iniquity of the Fatters upon the children unto the third and fourth generation of them that hate Me;and showing mercy unto thousands of them that love Me,and keep My commandments.

III

Thou shalt not take name of the Lord thy God, in vain;For the Lord will not hold him gulitless that taketh His name in vain.

IV

Remember the Sabbath day,to keep it holy. Six days shalt thou labor,and do all thy work but the seventh day is the Sabbath of the Lord thy God:in it thou shalt do not do [illegible] work,[illegible] nor thy son nor thy daughter, thy man servant nor thy maid servant,nor thy cattle, nor thy stranger that is [illegible] thy gates:for in six days the Lord made [illegible] the sea,and all that in them is, and rested the seventh day:Where fore the Lord blessed the Sabbath day,andhallowed it.

V

Honor thy father and thy mother: that thy days may be long upon the land which the Lord thy God giveth thee.

VI

Thou shalt not kill.

VII

Thou shalt not commit adultery.

VIII

Thou shalt not steal.

XI

Thou shalt not bear false withness against thy neighbor.

X

Thou shalt not covet thy neighbor's house, thou shalt not covet thy neighbor's wife,nor his man servant,nor his maid servant,nor his ox,nor his ass, nor anything that is thy neighbor's.

[Exodus 20:3-17]

Love to God

Love to man

PREFACE

From the beginning this has always been about the exceeding bright light which is shining from Christ in heavenly vision. I was, from the first day, arrested and apprehended by His brightness, the hiding of His Power, the bright beams shining from the pierced side of my Redeemer Kinsman, Who became us to give us true Sonship in Him.

My purpose in writing this book is born of a consuming passion to open before the world this great Light. In the earlier days I did not understand what all this meant, I only knew that I was captured by the bright heavenly vision of Christ. Now it has become very clear that this Light is Christ essentially – The Testator, Mediator, and Messenger of the New and Everlasting Covenant – Eternal Life Himself and the Righteousness of God.

This book is written that you may know Him Who is the Truth in all His fullness. In beholding Him, in contemplating this great revelation of the Lamb slain, we are changed into His image and prepared for the trying hour the remnant people of God are soon to enter into. The hour of the judgment of Him is come. In this time, His bride will make up her mind that she desires only her heavenly Bridegroom and forsakes all earthly, carnal considerations by the revelation of Jesus Christ (1 Peter 1:13). To know Him is Everlasting Life, which begins when we receive, in His fullness, Christ our Righteousness.

CHAPTER ONE

A COVENANT OF RIGHTEOUSNESS

God's Righteousness: The Hope of Israel

Greetings from one whom God has chosen to receive and share His message. I was given a charge from Jesus in 2006 to believe His message made plain upon the tables (Hab. 2:2) and hold it fast until the end. The message is Jesus Christ our Lord essentially—our Lord and Savior in character: the Righteousness of God (see Rom. 3:21, 22). This is a last days' message written to and seeking the Israel of God for the purpose that "the mystery of God" should be finished (see Rev. 10:7). The mystery of God is God manifested in human flesh (see 1 Tim. 3:16), even as it was in Christ Jesus. This demonstration of God's divine nature manifested in human flesh once again, yet soon to be manifested in an entire righteous nation of God, will close the long-standing controversy between Christ and Satan. This was always the grand climax of the plan of redemption.

"To whom God would make known what is the riches of the glory of *this mystery among the Gentiles*; which is Christ in you, the hope of glory" (Col. 1:27) (emphasis added).

Jesus Christ overcame the devil during His walk upon the earth, but this did not close the controversy. The devil shifted his accusations against the character of God, saying that—while Christ may have overcome his wiles—God's people Israel are yet subject to the bondage of sin and therefore, according to the adversary, under his dominion. Christ has purposed to gain and show forth a righteous nation of Israel before the end comes, even while the devil still reigns in this world of sin.

"*Jesus Christ overcame the devil during His walk upon the earth, but this did not close the controversy. The devil shifted his accusations against the character of God.*"

To see God triumph, first in Christ—the Firstfruits—then through His people was always the great desire of the holy men of old; their ardent purpose was always the Righteousness of God and the vindication of God's character before men and angels (see Exod. 32:12, 13; Josh. 7:9; Isa. 11:9, 60:21, 64:1, 2; Ezek. 36:20–38; Dan. 7:22; Hab. 2:14, 3:2; Mal. 4:2, 3). This righteousness was first revealed to the holy patriarchs and then more explicitly to the Jews, so that the righteousness of God should be declared to all nations. The precise timing and the way in which God would accomplish His goal was revealed to the prophet Daniel.

"And he said unto me, Unto two thousand and three hundred days; *then shall the sanctuary be cleansed*" (Dan. 8:14) (emphasis added).

And in Daniel 9:24, God reveals the scope of the victory to be gained at the close of the anti-typical (the true)

Day of Atonement when the sanctuary in heaven shall be cleansed.

"Seventy weeks are determined upon thy people and upon thy holy city, to finish the transgression, and to *make an end of sins*, and to make reconciliation for iniquity, and *to bring in everlasting righteousness*, and to seal up the vision and prophecy, and *to anoint the most Holy*" (emphasis added).

God first revealed to the Jewish nation the purpose He desired to achieve through them before the time of their probation as His special chosen nation should close. Through Messiah, they were *"to make an end of sins"* and *"to bring in everlasting righteousness,"* but this could not be because, as a nation, they rejected Him in whom alone their righteousness before God could be found. But righteousness is God's promise to all nations; God was revealing to the Jews His purpose for all mankind who would put their trust in Him! In Isaiah chapter 56, God revealed that, even during the Jewish dispensation, His covenant of grace and righteousness embraced all nations.

> **Thus saith the LORD, Keep ye judgment, and do justice: for my salvation is near to come, and my righteousness to be revealed. Blessed is the man that doeth this, and the son of man that layeth hold on it; that keepeth the sabbath from polluting it, and keepeth his hand from doing any evil. Neither let the son of the stranger, that hath joined himself to the LORD, speak, saying, The LORD hath utterly separated me from his people: neither let the eunuch say, Behold, I am a dry tree. For thus saith the LORD unto the eunuchs that keep my sabbaths, and choose the things that please me, and take hold of my covenant; Even unto them will I give in mine house and within my walls a place and a name better than of sons and of daughters: I will give them an everlasting name, that shall not be cut off. Also the sons of the stranger, that join themselves to the LORD, to serve him, and to love the name of the LORD, to be his**

> **servants,** ***every one that keepeth the sabbath from polluting it, and taketh hold of my covenant;*** **Even them will I bring to my holy mountain, and make them joyful in my house of prayer: their burnt offerings and their sacrifices shall be accepted upon mine altar; for mine house shall be called an house of prayer for all people. The Lord GOD which gathereth the outcasts of Israel saith, Yet will I gather others to him, beside those that are gathered unto him.** (Isa. 56:1–8) (emphasis added)

The Scripture says that God's salvation was near to come, and that is the same as His righteousness which was being revealed. While God has made provision for the salvation of all people who would come to Him and receive the gift of His righteousness by taking hold of His Covenant, He plainly declares that these also will keep His seventh-day Sabbath in honor of Him as their Creator and as a memorial of His mighty power as revealed in the creation of all things in heaven and in earth, the seas and all that in them is. Only those who enter God's covenant of salvation can keep the seventh-day Sabbath without polluting it; this can only be by faith in His word, for there is no other way that His Shabbat is revealed.

God's righteousness is not for those who *choose* willful transgression and disregard His ways, as this is not the spirit of the faith that lays hold on God's righteousness. The righteousness of God is our salvation and this is the everlasting covenant (see Gen. 17:7; Jer. 31:33; Heb. 10:16). It is God's promise of righteousness, which is His Own eternal, everlasting life (see Gal. 3:14; Acts 1:4, 5; Acts 2:33). God's great power—His eternal, everlasting life that He has promised to give us in His covenant and which we may take hold of by faith—is the righteous character of God. We are to be made partakers of His divine nature; we are to be sharers of His GLORY!

> **And [Moses] said, I beseech thee,** ***shew me thy glory*****. And (the Lord) said, I will make all my goodness pass before**

> **thee, and *I will proclaim the name of the LORD before thee*; and will be gracious to whom I will be gracious, and will shew mercy on whom I will shew mercy....And the LORD descended in the cloud, and stood with him there, and *proclaimed the name of the LORD*. And the LORD passed by before him, and proclaimed, The LORD, The LORD God, merciful and gracious, longsuffering, and abundant in goodness and truth, Keeping mercy for thousands, forgiving iniquity and transgression and sin, and that will by no means clear the guilty; visiting the iniquity of the fathers upon the children, and upon the children's children, unto the third and to the fourth generation. And Moses made haste, and bowed his head toward the earth, and worshipped.** (Exod. 33:18, 19; 34:5–8) (emphasis added)

God's glory is His character, perfectly proportioned, balancing the seemingly opposite prerogatives of His attributes of mercy and justice, which is the essence of His power and divinity. To be made partakers of the divine nature of God—His righteousness—has been the great desire of all holy and faithful believers since the fall of Adam, and it is still presented to us as our hope of glory (see Col. 1:27)!

> *"God's glory is His character, perfectly proportioned, balancing the seemingly opposite prerogatives of His attributes of mercy and justice."*

To the apostle John was revealed a glorious vision wherein the people of God are finally and fully to receive this great outpouring of God's power in His character, manifested so fully in the last days; behold, the Angel of Revelation 18:1:

"And after these things I saw another angel come down from heaven, having great power; and the earth was lightened with *His glory*" (Rev. 18:1) (emphasis added).

This is a glorious vision of the Holy Spirit of Christ, coming down as when Christ descended upon mount Sinai to reveal

His righteous law—but here He does not come down to write His law in stone but to fulfill His New Covenant Promise:

"This is the covenant that I will make with them after those days, saith the Lord, ***I will put my laws into their hearts, and in their minds will I write them*****; And their sins and iniquities will I remember no more. Now where remission of these is, there is no more offering for sin"** (Heb. 10:16–18) (emphasis added).

The Snake on the Pole

This is the glory of the Lord when His character is written in the hearts of His people—the righteousness of God and eternal life. But how is this glorious salvation to be obtained? The way into the Holiest of all, to lay hold upon God's covenant and the righteousness of God is by faith in Christ and His blood (see Rom. 1:17; Eph. 2:8; Rom. 3:24,25). But there is a great object lesson which Jesus, Yahushuwah Himself, made reference to when explaining how we must obtain the righteousness

The righteousness which is of faith speaks to us in this manner – Look and Live

that will enable us to enter into His kingdom; we must give attention to this object lesson at this time.

"And as Moses lifted up the serpent in the wilderness, even so must the Son of man be lifted up: That whosoever believeth in him should not perish, but have eternal life" (John 3:14, 15).

That we may know the working of faith that brings us salvation, Jesus points us to the snake on the pole that Moses lifted up in the wilderness: a picture and lesson of righteousness by faith. Christ is the righteousness of God, and the snake on the pole was a symbol of Him. The snake on the pole was a condensed object lesson and prophecy teaching the great truth of the Hebrew sanctuary and of Christ. The snake was made of brass which caused the Hebrew mind to think of the brazen altar of burnt sacrifice; this was where the lamb sacrifices were consumed by fire and sin was transferred to the sanctuary by the blood of the offerings being smeared on the horns and poured out at the bottom of the brazen altar (see Exod. 27:1, 2; Lev. 4:34). Sin and death were there blended with life and salvation at the bronze altar of burnt sacrifice.

> *"The snake on the pole was a condensed object lesson and prophecy teaching the great truth of the Hebrew sanctuary and of Christ."*

So when the Israelites murmured against God, were disobedient, and were being bitten by poisonous serpents in the wilderness, they were deserving of death. But, in His mercy, God commanded Moses to lift up a bronze serpent. The very agent of death to the Israelites, the snake, was to be covered in brass and lifted up on a pole to be the agent of their healing. So in like manner, Christ, **"...the Lamb slain from the foundation of the world"** (Rev. 13:8), clad His humanity—**"... in the likeness of sinful flesh"** (Rom. 8:3) —with the divinity of His righteous character, and was lifted up on the cross. God **"made him to be sin for us, who knew no sin; that we might be made the righteousness of God in him"** (2 Cor. 5:21).

So Moses was commanded to make a brazen snake and lift it up on a pole; all that the Israelites, who were dying from being bitten by deadly poisonous serpents, had to do was to look upon that brazen snake to be healed. Their obedience to the provision God had made brought them instant healing and a type of salvation, for within minutes they would have died if they did not look to the brazen snake. This object lesson, which Christ directs us to focus our attention on (John 3:14) makes plain the essence of saving faith. The Israelites knew there was no healing efficacy in that bronze snake—the healing clearly came from Yahuwah their God. But, in order to be saved from death, they must accept the chosen instrumentality and the way Christ had chosen and declared unto them for their salvation. To slight this instruction, to not hearken, to forsake, to doubt or murmur was to choose death in that time of crisis. But to look in faith to the snake on the pole was to bring salvation near and receive life and healing from God! This is the essence of saving faith—to hang our helpless souls upon the word that Christ speaks to us to be saved:

"It is the spirit that quickeneth; the flesh [or material, carnal things of earth] profiteth nothing: the words that I speak unto you, *they are spirit, and they are life*" (John 6:63) (emphasis added).

True Righteousness

True righteousness by faith does not seek to make void the law of God, which are Christ's words. The righteousness we must have must be witnessed to by the law and it causes us to walk and abide in the law (see Matt. 7:24; John 15:10). The true faith and the true Messiah—true Righteousness—does not attempt to destroy the law, but fulfills it.

"Think not that I am come to destroy the law, or the prophets: I am not come to destroy, but to fulfil. For verily I say unto you,

Till heaven and earth pass, one jot or one tittle shall in no wise pass from the law, till all be fulfilled" (Matt. 5:17, 18).

"The LORD is well pleased for his righteousness' sake; ***he will magnify the law*****, and make it honourable"** (Isa. 42:21) (emphasis added).

We are now in the last days, and God is seeking to gather in one His elect, His righteous nation: the Israel of God. The prophets foretold that God would establish a waymarker– a sign to mark out the way to follow, a standard, called an ensign or a banner, so that those who would join God's righteous nation could look for and seek it.

"And he shall set up an ensign for the nations, and shall assemble the outcasts of Israel, and gather together the dispersed of Judah from the four corners of the earth" (Isa. 11:12) (also see Isa. 5:26, 11:10, 49:22, 59:19 and 62:10, where a standard is the same as an ensign).

In the Scriptures the lifting up of an ensign was a flag or a standard around which the people were to gather. Often the ensign or banner would have some meaningful symbols or words that signified a unity of identity or purpose. Anciently, an ensign was a standard, often lifted up on a pole, behind which an army would assemble its troops, and thus it became a focal point for the soldiers preparing for battle. It is interesting to note that when God instructed Moses to make the brazen snake, he was to set it upon a "pole" which is the same Hebrew word that is used for "ensign" or "standard."

In the New Testament, Paul mentions these Scriptures from Isaiah of an ensign and applies them to Christ.

"And again, Esaias saith, There shall be a root of Jesse, and he that shall rise to reign over the Gentiles; in him shall the Gentiles trust" (Rom. 15:12).

Here Paul was quoting from Isaiah 11:10, which says, **"And in that day there shall be a root of Jesse, which shall stand for an ensign of the people; to it shall the Gentiles seek: and** ***his rest shall be glory*****"** (Isa. 11:10, KJV margin).

Please note that it is Gentiles (the unrighteous, who have not the righteousness of God) who are to seek to the standard of Jesus Christ. Both Jews and Gentiles have been shown to be in the bondage of sin. All of mankind can only gain the righteousness of God by assembling under that ensign and expressing faith in Jesus Christ.

A Vision for Our Time

To our great surprise and amazement God has purposed , once again at the end of time, to lift up an ensign of Jesus Christ, even as Moses lifted up the snake on a pole in the wilderness. We declare the sacred message that the directions from the Commander of the Lord's hosts to make this ensign and His command for us to set it forth before the people is found in the vision of the prophet Habakkuk.

"And the LORD answered me, and said, Write the vision, and make it plain upon tables, that he may run that readeth it. ***For the vision is yet for an appointed time, but at the end it shall speak, and not lie*****: though it tarry, wait for it; because it will surely come, it will not tarry. Behold, his soul which is lifted up is not upright in him: but** ***the just shall live by his faith*****"** (Hab. 2:2–4) (emphasis added).

It was after obeying these instructions of writing the vision and making it plain upon the tables that the message was given to me to believe His message and faithfully hold it fast. So in faith and obedience to these commands from my Master and the great Shepherd of the flock of God, I must lift up the ensign and explain to you the interpretation from the book of Habakkuk.

Habakkuk was told to "write the vision and make it plain upon the tables" (Hab. 2:2). But how are we to know which vision to make plain? Understand that in the very next chapter, Habakkuk was given an extraordinary vision of Jesus Christ in the glory of His second coming.

"God came from Teman, and the Holy One from mount Paran. Selah. His glory covered the heavens, and the earth was full of his praise. And his brightness was as the light; ***he had horns coming out of his hand: and there was the hiding of his power*****"** (Hab. 3:3, 4) (emphasis added).

This is a most glorious vision of our Lord and Saviour, and it is also a parallel vision of the coming of the angel of Revelation 18:1, who lightens the earth with his glory, for Habakkuk was also shown:

"For the earth shall be filled with the ***knowledge of the glory of the LORD*****, as the waters cover the sea"** (Hab. 2:14) (emphasis added).

This writing of the vision and making it plain upon the tables is revealed to be a world-wide work, and it has special significance in the finishing of the mystery of God under the mighty power of the angel of Revelation 18:1. It is a vision of Christ: a vision of faith, of blood, spirit, and law magnified. To understand how this is revealed in the Scriptures previously quoted from the book of Habakkuk, look at the marginal reference in the KJV for Habakkuk 3:4.

> "*This writing of the vision and making it plain upon the tables is revealed to be a world-wide work, and it has special significance in the finishing of the mystery of God.*"

"He ***had bright beams coming out of His side*****: and there was the hiding of His power"** (Hab. 3:4, KJV margin) (emphasis added).

This is one of the most sacred revelations in the entire canon of Scripture; this vision is one of the most glorious and bright pictures of Christ recorded in the Holy Bible! To Habakkuk was given a vision of Christ lighting the whole world with His glory. But from whence is this glorious light issuing? It is pouring forth, shining from His pierced side; that same pierced side from whence flowed the crimson stream that reconciled man to God![i] What is more, the Word of God declares that *there* in His pierced side is the Savior's glory; *there is the hiding of His power* (Hab. 3:4)!

Now, we have identified assuredly the vision Habakkuk was given that was to be made plain upon the tables. But what are these tables on which the vision of Christ is to be made plain? The Hebrew word used here for "tables" is *luach*. In every instance where *luach* is translated "tables" in the KJV, it is referring to the tables of the Ten Commandments. So remembering that since Sinai is referenced at the beginning of the vison (see Hab. 3:3) and *luach* is most often written concerning God's covenant, the Ten Commandments, therefore I concluded that the vision of Christ was to be made plain upon the two tables of the Ten Commandments. But how do you make one vision of Christ plain upon the two tables of the Law?

The singular and glorious focal point of the vision of Christ as seen by Habakkuk the prophet is that the bright beams of light are issuing from Christ's pierced side, even in the glory of His second coming, after His sanctuary ministration in heaven is completed. When we see Christ's pierced side in glory we are instantly reminded of how and where His precious side was pierced —He was pierced on the cross of Calvary. Therefore, we have two manifestations of Christ's sacrifice concerning His pierced side: we see His pierced side upon the cross and in glory. The tables of the Ten Commandments can be summarized as "love to God" (referencing the first four commandments on the first table) and "love to man" (referencing the last six commandments on the second table). The vision of Christ upon the cross, with blood and water (see John 19:34) pouring forth from His pierced side in two copious streams for the salvation of perishing man, is the vision to be made plain upon the second table: the greatest manifestation of Love to man.

"Greater love hath no man than this, that a man lay down his life for his friends" (John 15:13).

And the glorious vision of Christ with bright beams coming from His side (declared to be the *hiding* of His power in Hab. 3:4) is the vision and fulfillment of the first table: love to God (shown by God's people forsaking sin by the indwelling of Christ's Spirit so that the sanctuary in heaven can be finally cleansed and the Lamb set free). This is the ensign of Christ that is to be lifted up in the last days, calling on God's people to range under the banner! Christ's sacrifice and His eternally pierced side portrayed on the two tables of the Ten Commandments reveal that He alone is the fulfillment of the law and is the righteousness of God which all of the holy patriarchs and prophets sought for throughout this entire dispensation of grace—from the beginning when man first sinned to this present day.

In the vision Christ is portrayed as the fountain of all life and goodness and salvation, pouring out of Himself His sacred blood (the blood of the new and everlasting covenant—ministered in the heavenly sanctuary for the blotting out of our sins). Also coming from the wound in Christ's side is seen the water of Life — His flowing healing power in character. The bright beams of Christ's Righteousness shining from His pierced side in the vision are symbolic of His Own Holy Spirit — His original divinity and His Own Eternal Life which He makes us partakers of through faith in Him and His atonement, the provision of God for our salvation!

Habakkuk was further instructed that the vision was to accomplish a special purpose at an **"...appointed time..."** (Hab. 2:3) in the last days (**"...at the end..."** (Hab. 2:3) and, at that time, the vision would **"...speak, and not lie..."** (Hab. 2:3). Paul quotes this same verse from Habakkuk 2:3 in the book of Hebrews as referring to Christ: "**For yet a little while, and he that shall come will come, and will not tarry**" (Heb. 10:37)

The vision of Christ speaks and must teach us at this time—the time of the end—because the gospel has been distorted by many Christians who declare that God's law has been abolished, when, in fact, the law must remain to be a faithful witness to the righteousness of God and the true Messiah we are to receive—especially in these last days of earth's history.

Christ also must speak because—among the many who uphold that God's commandments, His judgments, and statutes remain to faithfully witness to the righteousness of God—many of these deny Christ's original, underived divinity, which, in doing so, means that they cannot escape the condemnation of the law because they deny the very righteousness of God.

Therefore, we are setting forth the gospel of righteousness which is to be lifted up and declared to all nations before the end comes. The gospel of Jesus Christ, not distorted, but declared to all nations in its right and proper setting is called in the Scripture **"...the everlasting gospel..."** (Rev. 14:6), and this is the message now being declared to you! Now we are lifting up the ensign of Christ made plain upon the tables of His law. It is a vision of Christ: a vision of faith—of His blood, His spirit, and His law magnified.

Habakkuk was further instructed concerning this last days' message of righteousness by faith.

"Behold, his soul which is lifted up is not upright in him: *but the just shall live by his faith*" (Hab. 2:4) (emphasis added).

The Just Shall Live by His Faith

This is the place in Scripture where, like no other, Paul establishes a foundation for his gospel doctrine of justification by faith (see Rom. 1:17, Gal. 3:11, Heb. 10:38). But notice here the end-time application of the message given to Habakkuk.

"The just[ified] shall *live* by HIS FAITH!" (Hab. 2:4) (emphasis added).

This is the faith of Jesus that we must have! And He is given to us also as a promise and a gift from the Most High, and this faith of Jesus is revealed to be a defining characteristic of the end-time saints who shall overcome the beast and his mark and all of the hellish powers on earth that are allied with the devil.

"Here is the patience of the saints: ***here are they that keep the commandments of God, and the faith of Jesus*****"** (Rev. 14:12) (emphasis added).

The faith of Jesus is the faith and experience of Christ when He walked on earth in His victorious life as a man, to gain for us salvation and to be our example. All of the works of Jesus were wrought by faith in His Father, God in heaven, because, when Jesus incarnated into humanity, He ... **"emptied himself..."** (Phil 2:7, ESV) of His original, unborrowed omnipotent power and omnipresence. Christ's walk and experience on earth, His righteous life in human nature, is the manifestation of God's character in human flesh, and this is the righteousness of God that the law of God demands. This is the ensign now to be lifted up to all nations, even as Moses lifted the snake on a pole in the wilderness.

There is much present truth revealed and taught by the vision that Habakkuk saw, now made plain upon the tables; **"... it shall, speak, and not lie..."** (Hab. 2:3). Now we are calling on **"...every nation, and kindred, and tongue, and people..."** (Rev. 14:6) to **'look and live'** (see Num. 21:8) in faith and receive the message: each feature of this message, and in its entirety, is essentially **"The LORD our RIGHTEOUSNESS"** (Jer. 23:6, 33:16) (emphasis added).

In the atonement, the character of God is revealed.

CHAPTER TWO

THE BLOOD OF HIS COVENANT

Christ Our Great High Priest

We see in the vision of Christ shown to the prophet Habakkuk, that upon the second table is Christ upon the cross, pouring out His sacred blood and cleansing water from His eternally pierced side in fulfillment of the Law of God: Love to man. This represents to us the beginning of His High Priestly ministration by His blood. When Christ died upon the cross of Calvary, He was crushed by the anguish caused by the totality of the sin of this world that had been laid upon Him. All sins that had ever been committed and shall ever be committed were laid upon our precious Jesus and He bore them to the death. When Christ revived and resurrected on the third day in fulfillment of the Scriptures, His sacrifice of redemption was complete: the way into the holiest of all was open and all mankind was now reconciled to God. Truly these sacred blessings were available to be experienced by those faithful believers who lived in former times before the death of Christ, because they were enlightened by the Holy Spirit to understand that Christ is **"...the Lamb slain from the foundation of the world"** (Rev. 13:8) and that the covenant of salvation through Christ was confirmed and active by the promise and oath of God (see Gal. 3:17). But certainly mankind entered a new epoch when the covenant was ratified by the shedding of Christ's blood upon Calvary (see John 19:30).

Then Christ ascended to heaven in order to gain assurance from the Father that His sacrifice had been accepted and that an abundant entrance would be ministered to His church to dwell and reign with Him forever in His everlasting kingdom at last (see 2 Peter 1:11; John 17:24). Having gained this assurance from the Father, Christ's work transitioned fully to become our great High Priest in the heavenly sanctuary for the finishing work of cleansing His church to prepare them to dwell with Himself, the Father and all the holy angels forever.

"We have such an high priest, who is set on the right hand of the throne of the Majesty in the heavens; A minister of the sanctuary, and of the true tabernacle, which the Lord pitched, and not man....For Christ is not entered into the holy places made with hands, which are the figures of the true; but into heaven itself, now to appear in the presence of God for us... ***once*** **in the end of the world hath he appeared to put away sin by the sacrifice of himself"** (Heb. 8:1, 2, and 9:24, 26) (emphasis added). (Also see Eph. 5:26, 27.)

Among Christians today, there is generally a great misconception concerning Christ's ministration in the heavenly sanctuary, and this error is consistent with and is derived from the error in Bible interpretation that teaches that

God abolished His law at the death of Christ. Consider the Scripture above that mentions that **"once"** Christ **"...appeared to put away sin by the sacrifice of himself"** (Heb. 9:26) Most Bible teachers interpret this "once" as referring to His death on the cross, but the context of this section in Hebrews 9 is concerning Christ's work in the heavenly sanctuary. How can it be understood then that Christ appeared "once" to minister in heaven? Paul uses this same thought of "once" concerning Christ's heavenly sanctuary ministry in another verse also in Hebrews chapter 9.

"Neither by the blood of goats and calves, but by his own blood *he entered in once* into the holy place, having obtained eternal redemption for us" (Heb. 9:12) (emphasis added).

The idea Paul is conveying in the epistle to the Hebrews with his focus on Christ's sacrifice (and His priesthood) as taking place "once" and being "one" is that it was effective to achieve the goal for which it is offered, unlike the many and oft-repeated sacrifices of the Levitical priesthood **"which could never take away sins"** (see Heb 10:1–4, 11). The many priests and sacrifices of the Levitical priesthood were typical of the only true sacrifice and priesthood of Christ.

Christ's one true sacrifice extends from Christ's incarnation, when He assumed humanity, to the cross of Calvary and continues until He shall **"appear the second time no longer to bear sin"** (Heb. 9:28). So **"...he entered in once into the holy place..."** in heaven (Heb. 9:12) (for Christ is still there today) until the sins of His church are **"...blotted out..."** and **"...there is no more sacrifice for sin"** (Acts 3:19, Heb. 10:18).

When this final phase of Christ's ministration is completed then the mystery of God shall be finished.

> *"Christ's one true sacrifice extends from Christ's incarnation, when He assumed humanity, to the cross of Calvary and continues until He shall "appear the second time no longer to bear sin" (Heb. 9:28)."*

"This is the covenant that I will make with them after those days, saith the LORD, I will put my laws into their hearts, and in their minds will I write them; And their sins and iniquities will I remember no more. Now where remission of these is, ***there is no more offering for sin*****"** (Heb. 10:16–18) (emphasis added).

Christ's ministration in the heavenly sanctuary is concerning our sins. He cannot close this ministration until a remnant of His people, who will be the end-time Israel of God, stop sinning as the revelation of Jesus Christ and the law of God are written in their hearts in fulfillment of the New Covenant promise (Heb. 10:16). It is only then, and not until that time is reached, that there can be **"…no more offering for sin"** (Heb. 10:18).

The Law of God Fulfilled in Heaven

The great error of many Bible teachers is the error of dispensationalism which teaches that God required good works of obedience to the law for the people to gain salvation before Christ died upon the cross, but after Christ died upon the cross, the church is now under grace and the law of God is abolished. This error has led to many distortions in how many Christians interpret the Scriptures and of Christ's ongoing ministry in heaven for His people.

In the many Scriptures in which it seems as if Paul is teaching that God's law is abolished (see 2 Cor. 3:7, Eph. 2:15, Col. 2:14), he is actually addressing the generally taught error of the Jews that led them to try to gain salvation through works of the law: which is to try to meet the demands of the law by their own unaided efforts in an attempt to produce righteousness. (Paul understood that this is a problem of sinful human nature, not simply a problem of the Jews and their Old Covenant ceremonial practices.) This error was so engrained in the Jews' thinking that Paul used the strongest language he could to show that salvation and righteousness can only come through Jesus Christ, apart from our performance and obedience to God's law.

> **Now we know that what things soever the law saith, it saith to them who are under the law: that every mouth may be stopped, and all the world may become guilty before God. Therefore by the deeds of the law there shall no flesh be justified in his sight: for by the law is the knowledge of sin. But now the righteousness of God without the law is manifested, being witnessed by the law and the prophets; Even the righteousness of God which is by faith of Jesus Christ unto all and upon all them that believe: for there is no difference: For all have sinned, and come short of the glory of God; Being justified freely by his grace through the redemption that is in Christ Jesus: Whom God hath set forth to be a propitiation *through faith in his blood*, to declare his righteousness for the remission of sins that are past, through the forbearance of God; To declare, I say, at this time his righteousness: that he might be just, and the justifier of him which believeth in Jesus.** (Rom. 3:19--26)

But we can show just as conclusively that Paul was careful to maintain the claims of God and His law upon every believer:

"For it makes no difference whether or not a man has been circumcised. *The important thing is to keep God's commandments*" (1 Cor. 7:19, NLT) (emphasis added).

"Do we then make void the law through faith? God forbid: yea, we establish the law" (Rom. 3:31) (emphasis added).

The subject of whether God's law remains active or if it has been abolished requires careful, Spirit-led study. It is true that the *earthly expression* of the ceremonial portions of God's law have been done away with—that is, God no longer requires or accepts animal sacrifices or an earthly priesthood in an earthly temple made by human hands in an earthly Jerusalem. But understand carefully that the reality of the ceremonial portions of God's law have not been abolished because the things that were indeed commanded by God to be performed on earth, which were examples and shadows of their true heavenly counterparts, are performed and being fulfilled in their true purpose by Christ in the heavenly sanctuary above!

"Think not that I am come to destroy the law, or the prophets: I am not come to destroy, but to fulfil. For verily I say unto you, Till heaven and earth pass, one jot or one tittle shall in no wise pass from the law, till all be fulfilled" (Matt. 5:17, 18).

"For Christ is not entered into the holy places made with hands, which are the figures of the true; but into heaven itself, now to appear in the presence of God for us" (Heb. 9:24).

Verily, verily the ceremonial law of God is not abolished but is being fulfilled in heaven by Christ, called in scripture **"...the Lamb slain..."** (Rev. 13:8). There is a sanctuary in heaven, within the city of God — the heavenly Jerusalem (see Rev. 3:12). There Christ is installed and consecrated as our great High Priest, ordained to offer His gifts and sacrifices and mediate the new (and everlasting) covenant for us (see Heb. 4:14 and 8:3, 6)!

In the Holy Scriptures, new covenant believers are directed to center our hope of righteousness within the veil of the heavenly sanctuary.

> **For when God made promise to Abraham, because he could swear by no greater, he sware by himself....That by two immutable things, in which it was impossible for God to lie, we might have a strong consolation, who have fled for refuge to lay hold upon the hope set before us:** ***Which hope we have as an anchor of the soul, both sure and stedfast, and which entereth into that within the veil*****; Whither the**

forerunner is for us entered, even Jesus, made an high priest for ever after the order of Melchisedec. (Heb. 6:13, 18–20) (emphasis added)

Entering within the Veil

The promise to Abraham, which was confirmed by the oath of God, is the everlasting covenant—the hope of the righteousness of God—which is described in Scriptures as **"the hope set before us"** (Heb. 6:18) which we are to lay hold of by faith. (This is the same provision extended to the Gentiles in Isaiah chapter 56—to take hold of God's covenant and keep His seventh-day Sabbath, as we discussed in Chapter One). But we are further told that this hope is **"an anchor of the soul"** (Heb. 6:19). But where does this anchor hold **"both sure and steadfast"** (Heb. 6:19)? The Scriptures reveal that our hope of righteousness, which is our anchor against the wiles of the devil, is accomplished by entering **"within the veil"** (Gal. 5:5, Heb. 6:19) of the temple of God in heaven to stand by the side of Jesus—yea, rather to abide in Him by faith! (See John 15:4, 5). We must enter into the Most Holy Place of the heavenly sanctuary (we enter in by faith) to behold Him. We must declare the present truth message at this time: The Lamb of God still sheds His sacred blood as He ministers in the heavenly sanctuary. He is both Priest and Sacrifice, Offerer and Offering....[ii]

"Having therefore, brethren, boldness to enter into the holiest by the blood of Jesus, By a *new* [*prosphatos*: newly slaughtered, freshly slain. *Strong's Greek Dictionary of the Bible*, #G4372 – 1 occurance] **and living way, which he hath consecrated for us, through the veil, that is to say, his flesh; And having an high priest over the house of God; Let us draw near with a true heart in full assurance of faith, having our hearts sprinkled from an evil conscience, and our bodies washed with pure water"** (Heb. 10:19–22) (emphasis added).

The Ministry in God's Sanctuary

Many Christians are unaware of what the Bible teaches concerning the services and ministry in God's sanctuary. In brief, the sanctuary is God's house, His dwelling place, many times also spoken of as the place where He set His name (character) to be made known to all nations (see 1 Kings 9:3, Jer. 7:11, 12). Anciently, before Jesus died on the cross, when God's people sinned (and sin is described in Scripture as transgression of God's law [1 John 3:4]), in order to be cleansed and forgiven, they were to bring a lamb without blemish (or another kind of unblemished living animal that God said He would accept as a sacrifice) to the sanctuary and confess their sins over the head of the sacrifice. The repentant sinner was then to cut the neck of the lamb himself, causing death to the innocent lamb who must perish as a substitute because the law of God decrees death as the penalty for their transgression of God's law. The priest would then come and collect the animal's blood and bring it into the sanctuary, where the priest would either sprinkle the blood before the veil (curtain-door) of the inner sanctuary or apply the blood to the horns of the altar of incense and finally pour the remaining

What was done in type in the ministration of the earthly tabernacle is done in reality in Christ's ministration in the heavenly sanctuary.

blood out at the bottom of the brazen altar of burnt sacrifice (this is detailed in Leviticus chapter 4). This service symbolized the transference of sin, first from the sinner to the sacrifice/substitute, then second, the transference of that sin from the substitute to the sanctuary itself via the blood of the sacrifice. While a substitute was accepted in the place of the sinner and he was on account of this pardoned, the sin was not canceled by the blood of the victim. It was the means God provided by which the sin was transferred to the sanctuary. Notice the significant and startling teaching of this object lesson: that God's house, the place where HIS NAME is manifested, is ultimately receiving the sins of His people!

As God's house accumulated the sins of His people day after day, it became necessary for a ministration by which God's house could be vindicated, justified, and cleansed from the sins accumulated there. You see, ultimately God takes responsibility for the sins of His professed children—those who believe and trust in Christ, His Son. (The unbelieving world requires that God do this—they blame Him, our Father, for the sins that His children commit and they claim that the sinful behaviors which they see in His people are a true representation of His character and His ways, in an attempt to justify their rejection of Him). But the sins and sinning of God's people is not what should be found in God's house, as these are not a true representation of His character. God desires His sanctuary, and thereby His name, to be cleared and cleansed, so that it may be justified from this misrepresentation our sins have caused. Therefore the law of God enjoins the services of the Day of Atonement, when not only God's sanctuary, but more importantly, His people—who currently are the source of the defilement—are cleansed from their iniquities and their sins are blotted out!

"Ultimately God takes responsibility for the sins of His professed children—those who believe and trust in Christ, His Son."

> ***For on that day shall the priest make an atonement for you, to cleanse you, that ye may be clean from all your sins before the LORD. It shall be a sabbath of rest unto you, and ye shall afflict your souls, by a statute for ever.* And the priest, whom he shall anoint, and whom he shall consecrate to minister in the priest's office in his father's stead, shall make the atonement, and shall put on the linen clothes, even the holy garments: And he shall make an atonement for the holy sanctuary, and he shall make an atonement for the tabernacle of the congregation, and for the altar, and he shall make an atonement for the priests, and for all the people of the congregation. And this shall be an everlasting statute unto you, to make an atonement for the children of Israel for all their sins once a year.** (Lev. 16:30–34) (emphasis added)

The Sacrifice Continues

For the Old Testament faithful, their participation in these God given ordinances was an expression of their faith in Messiah, Who was the object and substance of all these religious services. The ministrations of the earthly sanctuary were to teach us of Jesus Christ and the true ministration in the heavenly sanctuary. Just as the law of God continues as a faithful witness to God's righteousness, so likewise Jesus as our Lamb slain in heaven for the forgiveness of our sins, continues.

"And almost all things are *by the law* purged with blood; and without shedding of blood is no remission. *It was therefore necessary* that the patterns of things in the heavens should be purified with these; but the heavenly things themselves with better sacrifices than these" (Heb. 9:22, 23) (emphasis added).

Clearly Paul understood that it is necessary that the heavenly places be purified (cleansed) with better sacrifices than the blood of animals because it is required by the law of God; and by saying "better sacrifices," is meant the blood of Christ, which continues to flow for the forgiveness of our sins.

As anciently the sins of God's people were by faith placed upon the sin offering and through its blood transferred, in figure, to the earthly sanctuary, so now in the new covenant the sins of the repentant are by faith placed upon Christ and transferred, in fact, to the heavenly sanctuary by the blood of Christ. We must enter into the heavenly sanctuary by faith and confess our transgressions against God's holy law and His righteousness of love; but, as never before, we must see the continuing outflow of what the forgiveness of our sins cost. Christ must still bear our sins before they are transferred to God's house and that is why Jesus was shown to John in the Revelation as a Lamb slain.

"And I beheld, and, lo, in the midst of the throne and of the four beasts, and in the midst of the elders, *stood a Lamb as it had been slain…*" (Rev. 5:6) (emphasis added).

In the Old Testament Scriptures, when we read the words *forgive* or *pardon* they are translated from the Hebrew word *nasah* which means "to carry, to bear, to lift, to take away." For us to be forgiven of our sins, even today, Jesus must still bear those sins. God is long suffering, and He will "pass over" (as in the Passover) the transgressions of His people through their obedience in following the provision He made for our forgiveness and salvation, but, at the end of time, God has purposed to blot out all sin (see Acts 3:19). God's determination is **"to make an end of sins…and to bring in everlasting righteousness"** (Dan. 9:24), for even the Lamb will not bear our sins any longer when the sanctuary is cleansed.

"So also Christ was offered once to bear away the sins of many; and he will appear a second time, *not to bear sin*, but to bring salvation to those who eagerly await him" (Heb. 9:28, (Berean Study Bible) (emphasis added).

An End-time Revelation of the Lamb Slain

God made provision for the Reformers in the past who, while living up to the light that had shined upon them, had not this knowledge; they entered into the sanctuary by faith in Christ, as His ministration in the Holiest of all by His blood had not yet been revealed. But now in our generation, we are called to cooperate with God to **"bring in everlasting righteousness...."** (Dan. 9:24); we are to behold the Lamb, the righteousness of God.

"God having provided some better thing for us, that they without us should not be made perfect" (Heb. 11:40).

In these last days, Christ is sending us a message of great import to set before us the goal of gathering into the Israel of God by faith in His righteousness—not for our personal salvation; but that we may 'look and live', to honor God by believing in His righteousness imparted to us. Our purpose and motive for doing this can and should be to honor God by accepting His provision for us, which shall deliver the Lamb (see Obad. 1:21, where saviours is also deliverers in the KJV margin) from His ministration by His blood which has continued to this very hour.

"And I will pour upon the house of David, and upon the inhabitants of Jerusalem, the spirit of grace and of supplications: *and they shall look upon me whom they [and their sins] have pierced*, and they shall mourn for him, as one mourneth for his only son, and shall be in bitterness for him, as one that is in bitterness for his firstborn" (Zech. 12:10) (emphasis added).

This is the revelation of Jesus Christ and the righteousness of God (**"through faith in His blood"**). The time has come for the vision of Christ to **"speak and not lie"** (Hab. 2:3). Will you accept the truth concerning His blood shed for you today for the forgiveness of your sins, and one day soon to blot them out altogether from the heavenly sanctuary? By the power of God, do not refuse the revelation of Jesus Christ!

His Blood Is Speaking

Do not refuse the blood of sprinkling which is in heaven of a truth, just as the Scriptures declare.

"But ye are come unto mount Sion, and unto the city of the living God, the heavenly Jerusalem, and to an innumerable company of angels.... And to Jesus the mediator of the new covenant, and to the *blood of sprinkling, that speaketh* better things than that of Abel" (Heb. 12:22, 24) (emphasis added).

The blood of Jesus, for the purpose of "sprinkling" after the manner of the sanctuary, is just as literally present in heaven as the other things Paul mentions in the above Scripture. But more importantly for you and I at this time is what is written next by the Holy Ghost.

"See that ye refuse not him that speaketh*. For if they escaped not who refused him that spake on earth, much more shall not we escape, if we turn away from him that speaketh from heaven: Whose voice then shook the earth: but *now he hath

See that ye refuse not Him that speaketh from heaven.

***promised, saying, Yet once more I shake not the earth only, but also heaven*"** (Heb. 12:25, 26) (emphasis added).

It is the blood of sprinkling that speaketh (see Heb 12:24) and is speaking to us today! His message is "Behold Christ, crucified for our sins!" "Look at the cost of your sinning!" "See the long-suffering of our God!" "How long, O Christian, will you continue to partake of the dreadful institution of sin!"

The literal blood of Jesus, still shed and ministered in the heavenly sanctuary, is a revelation to our dull senses of the pain that, from its very inception, sin has caused the heart of God. "*See that ye refuse not him* that speaketh" (Heb. 12:25) (emphasis added).

This message is what is being proclaimed by the vision of Christ made plain upon the tables of God's law. Upon the second table of "Love to Man," Christ is made plain as the crucified One on the cross, and from His pierced side is pouring out His sacred blood and water for our cleansing. This is depicting when the literal fountain of His sacred blood, for the forgiveness of our sins, was opened.

"In that day there shall be a fountain opened to the house of David and to the inhabitants of Jerusalem for sin and for uncleanness" (Zech. 13:1).

Now behold, on the first table of "love to God," is made plain Christ in the glory of His second coming – with bright beams of light shining forth from that same pierced side! This is showing that Christ has closed His heavenly sanctuary ministry and He is returning for His church made pure, His bride **"...without spot or wrinkle"** (Eph. 5:27, GNB). Then, at that time, from His pierced side no longer is His sacred blood flowing for the forgiveness of the sins of His people (all their sins have been blotted out, the sanctuary is closed, and God's name has been vindicated!). At that time we may behold—and even now we may rejoice in vision—that issuing from His pierced side is no longer His crimson blood, but the bright shining of the glorious light of His power (see Hab. 3:4 KJV margin) representative of His eternal life and character!

This is the everlasting gospel of salvation in Jesus Christ, the Lamb Slain.

"**And I saw another angel flying through heaven, who *with blood* had the everlasting gospel to preach to them who dwell on the earth, and unto every nation and tribe, and tongue and people**" (Rev. 14:6, *Murdock's Translation of the Aramaic New Testament*) (Peshitta).

"...The hour of his judgment is come" (Rev. 14:7). The vision of Christ, made plain upon the tables, was purposed for an appointed time, **"...but at the end it shall speak, and not lie..."** (Hab. 2:3) (emphasis added).

"See that ye refuse not him that speaketh (Heb. 12:25), in plainness upon the tables and by His blood in heaven. Amen.

So Christ was once offered to bear the sins of many, and unto them that eagerly wait for His appearing shall He return, not to bear sin any longer, but to bring salvation.

CHAPTER THREE

THE PROMISE OF THE FATHER

The Covenant Fulfilled

We see in the vision of Christ shown to the prophet Habakkuk that upon the first table is presented Christ in the glory of His second coming to earth with bright beams of light shining out from His eternally pierced side, in fulfillment of the law: "love to God." This represents to us the time when God's people have been sealed by the Holy Spirit in latter rain power and Christ has closed the sanctuary in heaven after having blotted out the sins of His people. This is done in fulfillment of the everlasting covenant, revealed in Scripture to accomplish in us a righteousness that our obedience to the law could never do.

"This is the covenant that I will make with them after those days, saith the Lord, I will put my laws into their hearts, and in their minds will I write them; And their sins and iniquities will I remember no more. Now where remission of these is, there is no more offering for sin" (Heb. 10:16–18).

When the law of God is put into the hearts and written in the minds of Christ's people by His Holy Spirit, then **"...there is no more offering for sin"** (Heb. 10:18). Jesus will be for us the Lamb forever (see Rev. 22:1), but when He blots out the sins of His people, His sanctuary ministration will have been ended and He will no longer need to shed His sacred blood to forgive fresh sins committed by his people, for they then have been sealed to never sin again! Surely this is the hope of righteousness that all of the holy and faithful patriarchs and prophets have looked forward to from the beginning since Adam sinned.

This is the fulfilment of God's promise that all of God's faithful believers have waited and hoped for (see Gal. 5:5), that we become **"...partakers of the divine nature..."** and cease to crucify afresh Jesus the Lamb in heaven and **"...put Him to an open shame"** (2 Peter 1:4; Heb. 6:6). What makes this promise effectual in the lives of God's people is the mighty power that has been hidden as it were (**"...There was the hiding of his power"** (Hab. 3:4), but is now shining from Christ's pierced side in the vision of Habakkuk.

The Very Life of God

The bright beams of light shine from Christ, from His heart—this is the power of His original life, His power in character which we are to receive in His fullness. It is the Holy Spirit, the very soul of the life of Christ.

"Is the law then against the promises of God? God forbid: for if there had been a law given which could have given *life*, verily *righteousness* should have been by the law. But the scripture hath concluded all under sin, that the promise by faith of Jesus Christ might be given to them that believe" (Gal. 3:21, 22) (emphasis added).

The goal of salvation is the righteousness of God (see Rom. 10:3, 4), which is the perfect character of Christ. This is what the law of God demands; this is the covenant God has given to His people. In the previous Scripture, Paul says that it is not possible that any work or obedience that man can render can gain for him the righteousness of God, but, in expressing that, Paul also reveals that this righteousness, which is sought for and which is necessary, is "life," even God's own life (reread Gal. 3:21)! So the righteousness of God is actually His person, His Soul—His life: the divinity of His character.

"The goal of salvation is the righteousness of God (see Rom. 10:3,4), which is the perfect character of Christ. This is what the law of God demands; this is the covenant God has given to His people."

The Promise of the Father

In the Scriptures is revealed the great promise of the Father, which is the same as the everlasting covenant: He promised to send us His only begotten Son to give His life as a sacrifice for the salvation of all who believe (see Gen. 3:15; Gen. 22:8; John 3:16). But the covenant for our salvation involves more than Jesus' incarnation into humanity to live a perfect life as our example and to die upon the cross as our substitute and to shed His blood for our atonement. The promise of the Father is to send us the Holy Spirit to make effectual the atonement of Christ; without this great power of His life to come into our hearts, the sacrifice of Christ would be of no avail.

"And, behold, I send the *promise of my Father* upon you: but tarry ye in the city of Jerusalem, until ye be endued with power from on high" (Luke 24:49) (emphasis added).

"And, being assembled together with them, commanded them that they should not depart from Jerusalem, but wait for the *promise of the Father*, which, saith he, ye have heard of me. For John truly baptized with water; but ye shall be baptized with the Holy Ghost not many days hence" (Acts 1:4, 5) (emphasis added).

"Therefore being by the right hand of God exalted, and *having received of the Father the promise of the Holy Ghost*, he hath shed forth this, which ye now see and hear" (Acts 2:33) (emphasis added).

This is so amazing that the Scriptures definitively reveal the promise of the Father to be the sending of the Holy Spirit to cleanse and energize the hearts of His faithful children! But truly the Bible just as conclusively reveals that the promise of the Father, which is the everlasting covenant, was to send and give us His Son Jesus to be our salvation.

"For unto us a child is born, unto us a son is given: and the government shall be upon his shoulder: and his name shall be called Wonderful, Counsellor, The mighty God, The everlasting Father, The Prince of Peace. Of the increase of his government and peace there shall be no end, upon the throne of David, and upon his kingdom, to order it, and to establish it with judgment and with justice from henceforth even for ever. The zeal of the LORD of hosts will perform this" (Isa. 9:6, 7).

The vision of Christ made plain upon the tables, wherein Christ will **"...speak and not lie..."** (Hab. 2:3), is proclaiming the message that the Holy Spirit comes from Christ and is Christ Himself: His Life and Spirit, the divinity of His character. This is the everlasting covenant, the blessing of Abraham, that we receive as Christ Himself in our hearts:

"Even the *mystery which hath been hid from ages and from generations*, but now is made manifest to his saints: To whom God would make known what is the riches of the glory of this mystery among the Gentiles; *which is Christ in you, the hope of glory*" (Col. 1:26, 27) (emphasis added).

"That *the blessing of Abraham* might come on the Gentiles through Jesus Christ; that we might receive *the promise of the Spirit* through faith" (Gal. 3:14) (emphasis added).

"*Now the Lord is that Spirit*: and where the Spirit of the Lord is, there is liberty" (2 Cor. 3:17).

The everlasting covenant was made from all eternity between the Father and the Son; they existed together for all eternity past. They covenanted that, if any of their creation should sin, Christ, God's Son, would give up the form of God and come to earth and die as a sacrifice and then be resurrected to exist as God in humanity forever. This infinite sacrifice was to show the character of the infinite God, the character of the Father and the Son.

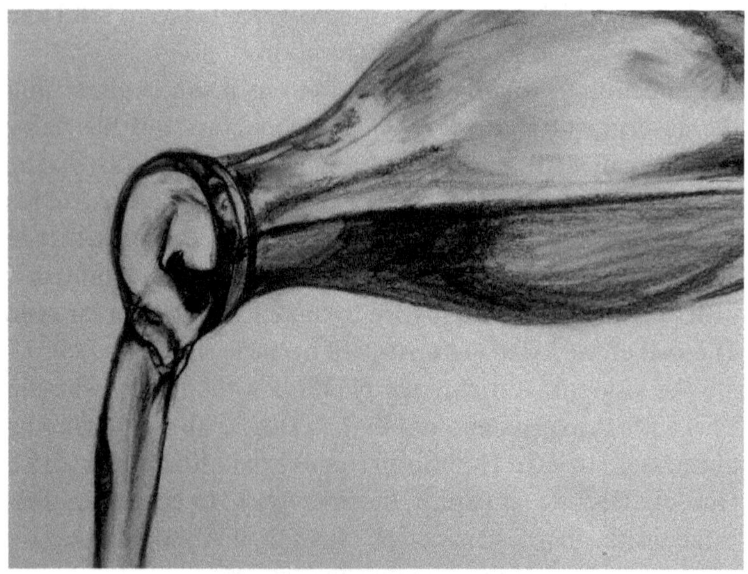

I am poured out like water...

When Christ incarnated and became human, He emptied himself of the form of God forever, because He would remain eternally bearing the form of humanity.

"*Let this mind be in you which was also in Christ Jesus*: Who, existing in the form of God, did not consider equality with God something to be grasped, but *emptied Himself*, taking the form of a servant, being made in human likeness" (Phil. 2:5–7, BSB) (emphasis added).

We are to receive the same mind of Christ, which enabled Him to sacrifice even His own life for our salvation, and to show the character of the living God. But how great was His sacrifice? We must understand His original estate before He came to earth to assume humanity.

The Spirit of Sacrifice

The attributes of Christ's deity in the form of God were omnipotent power, omniscience, and omnipresence. When He incarnated into humanity, Christ necessarily emptied Himself of these superhuman attributes, for He must become our example.

Cumbered with humanity, Christ could not be in all places personally; therefore, He told His disciples that it was altogether for their advantage that He should leave them and send the Holy Spirit to take His place (see John 16:7, 8). *The Holy Spirit is Christ Himself*, yet divested from and independent of His human personality. In sending the Holy Spirit, Christ would represent Himself in all places by His original omnipresence to encourage, guide, and live in the hearts of His faithful believers.

"I will not leave you comfortless: *I will come to you*" (John 14:18).

The Spirit of Christ would come in all the fullness of the original divine power Christ had as the Word, God in heaven, Who was with the Father. Dwelling in the hearts of His believers, He cleanses our hearts and purifies us from sin as the Spirit of Sacrifice (Isa 4:4), made available to us through the infinite sacrifice of His incarnation and the redeeming power of His atonement.

The Holy Spirit is as verily the life-blood (Soul) of Christ's deity in the form of God as is His sacred crimson blood that He sheds from His human body. Both are necessary for our salvation, both are provided for us in Christ's atonement for our sins, both His blood and His Holy Spirit come to us because of Christ's infinite sacrifice in the everlasting covenant and both come from Christ: our Righteousness.

Christ is the righteousness of God: He is Himself **"the resurrection and the life"** (John 11:25) we are to receive—the believer's assurance of the everlasting life promised to us. The promise of eternal life through God's covenant of faith is that we receive Christ's own Life, "...original, unborrowed, underived...,"[1] which He had in the form of God when He existed as the Word, God in heaven, Who was with the Father for all eternity past.

Jesus' Life: Original and Self-Existent

There are many who deny this. There are many who teach that the eternal life offered us in the covenant is the Father's life and that Christ did not exist always as a distinct and separate Person equal with the Father. They teach that, at some time far back in eternity past, the Father brought Christ into existence, which is how He is then His Son (see Luke 20:44) and that Christ did not exist as a separate distinct Person as long as the Father existed. These make and teach a great error, for in this they cannot have the righteousness of God, which is Christ's

---

[1] White, Ellen G. *The Desire of Ages*. Mountain View, CA: Pacific Press Publishing Association, 1898, p. 530.3.

original, unborrowed divinity and the believer's assurance of everlasting life.

The Father's life flows out to all creation through Christ. But it must be understood that the Father and Christ share the same original divine character, which all created beings with moral natures are to be made partakers of, which is truly the life of God. In the plan of redemption, wherein God and Christ covenanted from all eternity past, it was determined that Christ should be the conduit through which the glory (the character) of the Godhead is revealed. All inspired revelations of God and of Christ are to be understood in the context of the plan of redemption and the sacrifice of the Father and the Son.

The salvation of the human race has ever been the object of the councils of Heaven. The covenant of mercy through Christ existed from all eternity between God and Christ and is called *the everlasting covenant.* Just as surely as there was never a time when God did not exist, so surely there was never a moment when it was not the great purpose of the heart of God to manifest His grace to humanity. This grace is Christ's character revealed in His condescension in the plan of redemption and the Father giving up the only Being with whom He shared the same nature **"...in the form of God"** (Phil. 2:6, 7) for all eternity past.

"Now to him that is able to establish you according to my gospel and the preaching of Jesus Christ, ***according to the revelation of the mystery which hath been kept in silence through times eternal,*** **but now is manifested, and by the scriptures of the prophets, according to the commandment of the eternal God, is made known unto all the nations unto obedience of faith"** (Rom. 16:25, 26, ASV).

The divinity of Jesus Christ is original in Himself; it is not borrowed and is underived. Christ's Holy Spirit which was divested from His personality in humanity at His incarnation, is His original eternal life (see 1 John 1:1, 2 concerning

Christ being "eternal life" and then emptying Himself at the incarnation (Phil. 2:6, 7, ESV) and this is the righteousness of God we are to receive by faith. This is the everlasting covenant: that we "receive the promise of the Spirit" (see Gal. 3:14); to accomplish this, the scriptures testify that it is of necessity that the death of the Testator "be brought in" (Heb. 9:16 KJV margin). The Holy Spirit, the Righteousness of God, comes to us because of Christ's infinite, eternal sacrifice:

"For ye know the grace of our Lord Jesus Christ, that, though he was rich, yet for your sakes *he became poor*, that ye through his poverty might be rich" (2 Cor. 8:9) (emphasis added).

"Whereby are given unto us exceeding great and precious promises: that by these ye might be partakers of (Christ's) divine nature..." (2 Pet. 1:4).

Christ was "in the form of God" (Phil. 2:6) when He covenanted with the Father before the foundation of the world; then at His incarnation into humanity (which is forever and ever), His personality "in the form of God" *died*... Verily, the Testator of the Covenant, the pre-incarnate Christ, died the "second death" when He "emptied Himself" (Phil. 2:7 KJV margin) and assumed humanity—which is, as it pertains to the pre-incarnate Christ, an everlasting death—a death from which there is no hope of resurrection. This is the pledge (promise) that God has given to us that He will fulfill His word; "...for unto us (the) Son is given..." (see Isa. 9:6): Christ will bear human nature forever, that He may live in us by His "eternal Spirit" (Heb. 9:14; Eph. 2:22). (And inseparably connected with this truth is its counterpart: the blood of Jesus must of necessity "be brought in", into the Most Holy Place of the heavenly sanctuary, because God has ordained that the blood of sprinkling shall always signify the death of the Testator (see Lev. 17:11; Heb. 9:16-23,12:24).

In view of the great, immeasurable sacrifice of God, it is important to make an honest consideration: will you receive the righteousness of God? Ask yourself according to your faith and your understanding of the Word of God, is Jesus God? (See John 1:1, 2, Heb. 1:9). Do you receive that Christ, in the beginning, was God absolutely, entirely—in every essential capacity as you understand God in the highest sense (e.g., self-existent, life itself, the source of eternal life, having existed always and forever, omnipotent, omniscient. omnipresent: God)[iii] and, in that capacity as God, He was with God the Father from all eternity past, as long as the Father has existed?

If you receive this and the Holy Spirit of Christ, as the Spirit from His infinite sacrifice: the Soul of His life... then you receive the righteousness of God by **"...the faith of Jesus"** (Gal. 2:16; Rev. 14:12), which **"...will guide you into all truth..."** and salvation (John 16:13).

Is God One?

Through Moses it was revealed to mankind concerning the Godhead.

"Hear, O Israel: The LORD our God is one LORD: And thou shalt love the LORD thy God with all thine heart, and with all thy soul, and with all thy might" (Deut.6:4, 5).

The Jews always understood this revelation as teaching that there is literally and numerically one God in Heaven and there always had been. But their own Scriptures gave evidence that there was always more that was revealed concerning the Godhead than their traditional orthodox view, which is called *monotheism.*

"And God said, Let *us* make man in *our* image, after *our* likeness..." (Gen. 1:26–28) (emphasis added).

The Hebrew word translated as *God* in the Old Testament is "Elohim," which properly means "Gods", is the numerical plural of the Hebrew word *eloah* (which means *God*, singular). So from the beginning, the God of Israel was revealed as being more than one numerically. Then in Genesis 2 was this revelation concerning man and woman who were made in the image of God:

"Therefore shall a man leave his father and his mother, and shall cleave unto his wife: and *they shall be one flesh*" (Gen. 2:24) (emphasis added).

So the Scriptures in the first two chapters of Genesis reveal the true nature of the Godhead: that Deity is more than one numerically but they two are one in purpose, mind, and character. The Jewish understanding of the revelation so often repeated in Scripture that there is one God (again, *God* being the plural word *Elohim*) formed the basis of the orthodox understanding of the Godhead called *monotheism*, which is concerned with God being numerically one. But the Jews misunderstood many Scriptures and were in error about many things concerning the mystery of God.

We should more highly esteem the teaching of Messiah Himself, the Messenger of the Covenant (see Mal. 3:1–3), and His teaching concerning the nature of the oneness of God, more than we esteem what the Jews understood.

This is what the Messiah taught concerning the Oneness of God:

"And the glory which thou gavest me I have given them; *that they may be one, even as we are one*: I in them, and thou in me, that they may be made perfect in one; and that the world may know that thou hast sent me, and hast loved them, as thou hast loved me" (John 17:22, 23) (emphasis added).

Christ explains that the oneness, the unity, that He prays to exist between Himself and His disciples is the very same oneness, unity, that He and the Father share; and this unity, this oneness, does not destroy the personality of either of the individuals. They are one in purpose, in mind and character, and it is thus that God and Christ are One. According to Christ Himself, **"Yahuwah, our Elohim, is one Yahuwah"** (Deut. 6:4, Hebrew) is not meant to be understood as numerical oneness, as though there was numerically and literally one God, but the focus and glory is oneness in character **"between the two of them"** (Zech. 6:13, NRSV, Hebrew meaning)! This focus on the character of God is the great revelation to our world, the light of this world, which the enemy of souls is constantly working to misrepresent.

"*This focus on the character of God is the great revelation to our world, the light of this world, which the enemy of souls is constantly working to misrepresent.*"

Two Great Errors

Two great errors in Christology have come from the Christian church adopting the Jews' understanding of there being numerically one God (monotheism) and not receiving the truth as taught by Christ Jesus Himself about He and the Father being one.

In attempting to maintain the traditional, orthodox understanding that there was meant to be only, numerically one God, the Christian church soon found herself in a contradiction of doctrine when the revelation of Christ in the New Testament dawned upon mankind.

How could Christ be God, as the Bible teaches (see John 1:1, 2; Heb. 1:8), if there is only supposed to be one God?

So in response to this crisis brought on by the Christian church assuming the original Jewish error of orthodox monotheism, over time the Christian teachers and theologians formulated two competing theories, which are both errors in doctrine. These new theories were the church's attempt to incorporate Christ into the Godhead while maintaining the understanding that there must be numerically one God.

The first of these errors is the error of a consubstantial Godhead (called the *Trinity*) which teaches concerning God and Christ that, God the Father is the source Who begets Christ by an "eternal generation", thus producing the Son continuously. Human philosophy, many Latin and Greek terms and invented expressions, such as *hypostasis, subsistentia and homoouisios,* were necessary to arrive at this conclusion. This error of consubstantial oneness in the Godhead teaches that, while there are expressions in the Bible of Persons identified as the Father, the Son and the Holy Spirit, They are really of one single, undividable essence of divine Being —therefore, since Their essence of existence derives from the Father, They remain numerically one God. (The Trinity is declared by the Roman Catholic Church in their catechism to be the root doctrine from whence all of their other teachings, which they call *mysteries*, derive.)

The second of these errors that was developed by the Christian scholars and teachers to maintain the Jewish understanding that there is numerically one God was the error of what is historically called *Arianism* (or the closely related semi-Arian position). This teaching maintains that there is numerically only one God by outright denying that Christ is Deity at all. This error teaches that Jesus was created by God the Father in eternity past, so that God the Father is the one God and that Jesus is a created being and is therefore not considered divine. (This is a purely Arian position that but few espouse today.) But the more popular form of this teaching is what theologians call the *semi-Arian position*. The semi-Arian position teaches that, while Christ has a divine nature because He is the only "begotten" Son of God, at some point in eternity past Christ was literally birthed or derived from the Father. Therefore, as an article of faith, those who hold this view assert that Christ did not exist as a distinct Person from the Father for as long as the Father has existed, because, they say, in order for God to be the Father, His life must be antecedent to Christ's. The central pillar of this teaching is that Christ is the Son of God by having a beginning of existence.

So they teach with great emphasis that God the Father is "...the only true God..." (John 17:3), in the sense that Christ is not and was never a "true" God, because, they say, only the Father existed for all eternity past.

Both of these errors were formulated in an attempt to reconcile the ancient understanding of Jewish monotheism with the revelations of Christ, the Son of God, in the New Testament. Both of these errors teach that Christ's divinity, if He has any, is not original within Himself, but is borrowed or derived from the Father at Christ's earliest state of existence.

The truth of Scripture is that Christ's declaration, as the **"...only begotten Son..."** (John 1:18), is in reference to His infinite sacrifice in the everlasting covenant and His incarnation into humanity forever. This truth places emphasis on Christ choosing to demonstrate God's character of humility and self-sacrificial love in the covenant plan to save us. By contrast, the semi-Arian teaching places the focus of "the only begotten Son" on Christ being literally birthed or begotten by God the Father sometime in eternity past. This thinking is from pagan and Greek influences—which often represented their gods as having carnal relations and producing babies (man often attempts to explain the mystery of God by the confines of our temporal existence see Ps. 50:21) and denies that Christ existed as a separate and distinct Person with the Father for all eternity past, as is revealed in the Scriptures, especially in John 1:1, 2.

The result of these two great errors in Christology and the danger they pose to our faith are as follows: the doctrine of a consubstantial trinity prevents a full understanding of Christ's victory in His human nature because it doesn't allow that He emptied Himself of His super-human "omni" powers so that He could be our example by exercising faith in His Father's power to do the work (while He yet possessed His original divinity in His righteous *character*)[iv]. The consubstantial Trinity teaches that while Christ was on earth, He was of one substance or consisted of the same essential singular being as the Father, therefore having His "omni" powers retained within Himself, which is a status that cannot ever happen in us. But Scripture tells us that we are to be **"...partakers of the divine nature..."** (2 Peter 1:4)—that is, we are to be partakers of Christ's righteous character, like Adam had an opportunity to develop in Eden before he was tempted and fell.

The semi-Arian view of Christ, on the other hand, prevents the understanding of Christ's "...original, unborrowed, underived..." deity—that He was absolutely equal with the Father, *including duration of existence,* and is called in scripture **"...that eternal life..."** (1 John 1:2). Cutting short this understanding minimizes by that infinite degree His glory (and that of the Father). It lessens His sacrifice and condescension in forever assuming humanity and placing Himself in eternal subjection to God, Who, concerning *the Everlasting Covenant*, is His Father (see Heb. 1:5). God is love and, by His divine nature, He is a social Being; and social beings have a natural desire for sympathy and companionship which is only truly afforded by communion with another being having the same nature. In the everlasting covenant, which is the plan of redemption to show mercy to man and reveal the depths of

The names The Father and The Son are the heart of the Everlasting Covenant and intrinsically presage the infinite sacrifice of Christ and His Father which makes us true sons of God.

His love, the Father has given up the only One who could ever be like Himself **"...being in the form of God..."** (Phil. 2:6, 7). The Father is henceforth God alone: "**the only *true* God**" (John 17:3). This is eternal, unfathomable self-sacrificing love— Christ consented to be given to us; eternally to bear human nature and to sit upon the throne of Deity, with His Father, as the Lamb for all eternity (see Isa. 9:6; Rev. 22:1). The semi-Arian teaching eclipses this full understanding of Christ's condescension and the infinite sacrifice of the Father and the Son.

These two great errors in Christology prevent us from seeing the length of the living chain of mercy let down from heaven to save us. Each error cuts short one of the two ends of the mystical ladder that God revealed to Jacob in a dream as representing Christ and the basis of the everlasting covenant.

"And [Jacob] dreamed, and behold *a ladder set up on the earth, and the top of it reached to heaven*: and behold the angels of God ascending and descending on it" (Gen. 28:12) (emphasis added).

If this ladder is ever cut short, even by one rung, of reaching the very throne of God (in the highest sense) or if this ladder should in any way fail of reaching completely to the earth (so that sinful human beings could not step onto it and ascend it), then we would fail of the righteousness of God in the knowledge of God and our faith (see 1 John 5:20; Rom. 8:3, 4).

A Covenant of Just and Right Government

The understanding of God the Father and Jesus Christ existing together always, since the beginning, in oneness of character is the foundation of understanding the government of God (Yahuwah, the God of Abraham, Isaac, and Jacob) and the Light of this world. How we understand this first principle is central to how we understand the Sonship of Christ. If Christ is **"that eternal Life Who was with the Father"** (1John 1:2) for all eternity past, then His eternal Sonship is that of choice, trust, and faith in that He chose to die and give up "the form of God" and in its place retain human nature forever. If Christ's life is not original in Himself, but is generated or derived from the Father at His earliest state of existence, then He is the Son by nature, by being and substance — in which case the Child, in owing proper fealty for His existence, ought to obey His Father as a matter of duty... But what says the mind of God:

"**But I did not want to do anything without your consent, so that your goodness will not be out of compulsion, but by your own free will.**" (Phil. 14 BSB) — i.e. "lest it should wear even the semblance of constraint." Ellicott's Commentary for English Readers — to be clear of this 'semblance of constraint', Christ must be eternal and self-existent of His own right, original and underived.

This has direct bearing upon us and the knowledge of God, which is integral in how we receive salvation and assimilate what we understand to be the character of God. The true knowledge of God teaches that God the Father and Christ agreed upon the Everlasting Covenant for as long as God has existed. Christ is expressly called the Testator of the Covenant (see Heb. 9:16, 17). Therefore, in Christ's submitting as the Son in the Everlasting Covenant agreement between He and the Father is revealed a form of government in which the government derives its power to govern from the consent of the governed. In the beginning Christ, being the eternal Son of God and the Creator, represented all creation in Himself as choosing submission to the Father. So Christ gave the first example of the system of submission of which He was co-author:

"**And (Jesus) said unto them, the kings of the gentiles exercise lordship over them; and they that exercise authority upon them are called benefactors. But ye shall not be so: *but he that is greatest among you, <u>let him be as the younger</u>*; and he that is chief, as he that doth serve**" (Luke 22:25, 26).

"For unto us a child is born, unto us a son is given: and the government shall be upon *his* shoulder" (Isa. 9:6).

This is government by absolute consent of the subjects to serve others and the interests of the kingdom. So like as when Christ was baptized, He gives us the example we are to follow: "The Son" (John 3:35) means God consenting to be governed (see Eccl. 12:13). This arrangement can only be born of faith in God's eternal plan and love for the character of the Lord of the kingdom; and love cannot be commanded, only by love can love be awakened. Verily, for us to receive eternal 'sonship' (which is a truer translation of the Greek word "huiothesia," translated as "adoption" in the New Testament—read all these verses replacing "adoption" with 'sonship': Rom. 8:15, 8:23, 9:4; Gal. 4:5; Eph. 1:5) then we must also follow the example of Christ and die, that we may live life "more abundantly" (John 10:10) in the kingdom of the resurrected Son."

Therefore, in the Everlasting Covenant we are given the Promise of the Father, the Holy Spirit: the Spirit of Love and Sacrifice of Christ, to create us in the kingdom of God, not merely as subjects serving the Monarch, but as dear children of the royal family.

"And because ye are sons, God hath sent forth the Spirit of His Son into your hearts, crying, Abba, Father. Wherefore thou art no more a servant, but a son, and if a son, then an heir of God through Christ" (Gal. 4:6, 7).

"But as many as received *Him*, to them gave he power to become the sons of God, even to them that believe on his name" (John 1:12).

This point is crucial for all future happiness and was always God's original plan—that all the sons and daughters of God would consent and choose His government as the surest way to secure their eternal happiness in submission to the King:

> **And I beheld, and I heard the voice of many angels round about the throne and the beasts and the elders: and the number of them was ten thousand times ten thousand, and**

> **thousands of thousands; Saying with a loud voice, *Worthy is the Lamb that was slain* to receive power, and riches, and wisdom, and strength, and honour, and glory, and blessing. And every creature which is in heaven, and on the earth, and under the earth, and such as are in the sea, and all that are in them, heard I saying, Blessing, and honour, and glory, and power, be unto him that sitteth upon the throne, and unto the Lamb for ever and ever. And the four beasts said, Amen. And the four and twenty elders fell down and worshipped him that liveth for ever and ever.** (Rev. 5:11-14)

> *"This point is crucial for all future happiness and was always God's original plan—that all the sons and daughters of God would consent and chose His government as the surest way to secure their eternal happiness in submission to the King."*

If we would have Him, Jesus Christ has covenanted to be the Guarantor and Protector of our eternal good and well-being. God has promised: "**If you will keep [accept] My covenant**" (Exod. 19:5) (just as Abraham believed/accepted God's promise and God "**counted it to him for righteousness**" [Gen. 15:6])—then, upon your desire, "***I will be your God***" (Exod. 6:7, Lev. 26:12).

Christ is that Eternal Life

The vision of Christ is speaking at this time and He does not lie (see Hab. 2:3). Christ was shown to the prophet Habakkuk in the glory of His second coming, with bright beams shining forth from His pierced side and Heaven is declaring that there is the hiding of the power of God (see Hab. 3:4, KJV margin). The bright beams of light that shine into our world from Christ's pierced side are the Light of this world, the revelation of Jesus Christ. Every ray of divine light that has shined into our dark world has come from Christ, and we are enlightened by His Spirit, which is often called in Scripture, **"...the Holy Ghost..."** (Acts 1:8). The vision of Christ revealed through the prophet Habakkuk shows us that the Holy Spirit is the Spirit life-blood (as it were) of the pre-incarnate Christ when He was in **"the form of God":** *The Soul of His Life* (see *Review and Herald*, May 19, 1904, par. 1).

Because of this, I was compelled to address the long-standing, fundamental errors that have dominated Christian teaching and theology and which obscure the full revelation of Jesus Christ. The time has come for Christ to speak and to shine the true light: if we continue to believe and partake in one of these errors in Christology (consubstantial oneness or the semi-Arian idea that Christ was derived in eternity past) after the correcting light that God is shining upon us, then we reject the light which heaven is pleased to reveal to this final generation, and we deny the righteousness of God.

The righteousness of the covenant given to us to save our souls is Christ's Own eternal life which He had in Himself from the beginning, and which also He poured out in infinite sacrifice for us in the plan of redemption.

"In the beginning was the Word, and the Word was with God, and the Word was God. The same was in the beginning with God" (John 1:1, 2).

The Holy Scriptures reveal that, in the uttermost revelation of eternity past, "in the beginning," were: God the Word, who was with God the Father—two Gods who were and are "...one in purpose, mind and character...." Christ had His Own "... original, unborrowed, underived..." eternal life in Himself. It is after the incarnation, when Christ emptied Himself of the form of God (in which consisted His omnipresence) that we understand by the Scriptures that the Godhead is made up of a heavenly trio of three divine Persons: The Father, Christ in humanity, and the Soul of His Life—The Holy Spirit.

In a parallel revelation to John 1:1, 2 which was quoted previously, John was given this revelation by the Holy Ghost to further clarify:

"That *which was from the beginning*, which we have heard, which we have seen with our eyes, which we have looked upon, and our hands have handled, of the Word of life; (For the life was manifested, and we have seen it, and bear witness, and shew unto you *that eternal life, which was with the Father*, and was manifested unto us" (1 John 1:1, 2) (emphasis added).

This Scripture plainly teaches us that the eternal life promised us in the everlasting covenant is Jesus Christ Himself. Eternal life was not given to Jesus by the Father nor was it borrowed or derived from the Father; Jesus is declared to be **"that eternal life, which was *with* the Father"** (1 John 1:2) from the very beginning.

This is the revelation Lucifer hates and would feign deny—that Christ existed with the Father for as long as God has been, for all eternity past. As long as God has existed, the two of Them had been *"Face to Face"* (a proper rendering of the original Greek text translated in our Bibles as **"…the Word was with God…"** (John 1:1). Self-existence from all eternity is essential to the deity of Yahuwah our Elohim. Ironically, Lucifer desired God's power and authority, but not His character (see Isa. 14:12-14; Zech. 4:6). Yet of all God's mighty attributes, we know His character of self-sacrificing love is the supreme power of all earth and heaven (1 Cor. 12:31).

The revelation of Christ has come and now shines in the last generation. Oh, this day, receive the righteousness of God which is Christ's eternal life—His Spirit of self-sacrificing love, as promised to us in the everlasting covenant between Christ and His Father.

"And as Moses lifted up the serpent in the wilderness, even so must the Son of man be lifted up: That whosoever believeth in him should not perish, but have eternal life. For God so loved the world, that he gave his only begotten Son, that whosoever

believeth in him should not perish, but have [His Son's Own] everlasting life" (John 3:14–16) (emphasis added).

This message is what is being proclaimed by the vision of Christ made plain upon the tables of God's law. Upon the first table of "Love to God," Christ is made plain as glorified, coming in great power to claim His bride, His church: the end-time Israel of God. And from His pierced side is shining forth bright beams of His Life, and the Scriptures declare that this is where His power has been hiding (see Hab. 3:4 KJV margin). This is depicting the time after Christ has blotted out the sins of His people by shedding, one final time, His sacred blood and having sprinkled it upon the mercy seat in heaven to fulfill the law of the Day of Atonement (Lev. 16). Then our Fountain of all life and salvation, instead of pouring out His sacred blood, sheds forth bright beams of glorious light: representing the Source of the eternal life given to us for salvation in the everlasting covenant: Christ, our righteousness.

"And this is life eternal, that they might know thee the only true God, and Jesus Christ, whom thou hast sent" (John 17:3).

Eternal life is knowing the character of the Living God which the Father and Christ share. This can only be when Christ dwells in our hearts by faith (see Eph. 3:17) and the Spirit writes God's law in our hearts and minds (see Heb. 10:16). Receive ye eternal life; receive the message and Christ's Holy Spirit revealed to be the Spirit of sacrifice, which Christ sheds abroad for the salvation of all who believe (see Acts 2:33 and Rom. 5:5) and to gain a righteous nation: the Israel of God, who will very soon be sealed and cease to sin against God and the Lamb.

This is the first table of the law, "Love to God," fulfilled; this is the righteousness of God, now declared and made plain upon the tables of God's law that we may **"…run with patience the race that is set before us"** (Heb. 12:1). Let whosoever readeth and understandeth, **look at it and live** (Num. 21:8, NIV) and stand with the Israel of God (see Isa. 11:10, KJV margin).

"He had Bright Beams coming out of His side and there is the hiding of His Power" - The Spirit of Sacrifice.

CHAPTER FOUR

THE GATHERING TIME

God's Schedule

Having made known unto us the mystery of his will, according to his good pleasure which he hath purposed in himself: That *in the dispensation of the fulness of times he might gather together in one all things in Christ*, both which are in heaven, and which are on earth; even in him: In whom also we have obtained an inheritance, being predestinated according to the purpose of him who worketh all

> **things after the counsel of his own will: That we should be to the praise of his glory, who first trusted in Christ. In whom ye also trusted, after that ye heard the word of truth, the gospel of your salvation: in whom also after that ye believed, ye were sealed with that holy Spirit of promise, which is the earnest of our inheritance until the redemption of the purchased possession, unto the praise of his glory.** (Eph. 1:9–14) (emphasis added)

We are made to understand by the Scriptures that God works everything out in His will, in the plan of redemption according to His timetable, according to His schedule.

Paul declared in the Scriptures previously mentioned that Christ will gather all things in one (one in harmony, unity of purpose, mind, and character), both which are in heaven and on earth in Himself. When will this take place? The Scripture quoted tells us that Christ will gather all things in one, in Himself, in that dispensation of the fullness of times.

It is clearly revealed in the Holy Scriptures that God has a schedule of times in which He has planned for each of the steps and events to occur in the plan of redemption provided for us in the everlasting covenant.

There was a time planned, known only to God, when Christ was to come into the world.

"But *when the fulness of the time was come*, God sent forth his Son, made of a woman, made under the law, To redeem them that were under the law, that we might receive the adoption of sons" (Gal. 4:4, 5) (emphasis added).

> "*It is clearly revealed in the Holy Scriptures that God has a schedule of times in which He has planned for each of the steps and events to occur in the plan of redemption.*"

After His baptism, anointing by the Holy Ghost, and victory over the devil in the wilderness of temptation, Christ announced that the time had come for Him to open His public ministry and preach the gospel, as it was foretold by Daniel the prophet (see Dan. 9:25).

"Now after that John was put in prison, Jesus came into Galilee, preaching the gospel of the kingdom of God, And saying, *The time is fulfilled*, and the kingdom of God is at hand: repent ye, and believe the gospel" (Mark 1:14, 15) (emphasis added).

Christ died upon the cross the very year pointed out by Daniel the prophet (see Dan. 9:26, 27), on the day of Passover on God's sacred calendar and at the very hour that the evening sacrifice was offered.

"And it was about the sixth hour, and there was a darkness over all the earth until the ninth hour. And the sun was darkened, and the veil of the temple was rent in the midst. And when Jesus had cried with a loud voice, he said, Father, into thy hands I commend my spirit: and having said thus, he gave up the ghost" (Luke 23:44–46).

And again.

"For *at just the right time*, while we were still powerless, Christ died for the ungodly" (Rom. 5:6, BSB) (emphasis added).

The Holy Spirit was poured out upon the day of Pentecost in God's sacred calendar.

"And *when the day of Pentecost was fully come*, they were all with one accord in one place. And suddenly there came a sound from heaven as of a rushing mighty wind, and it filled all the house where they were sitting. And there appeared unto them cloven tongues like as of fire, and it sat upon each of them. And they were all filled with the Holy Ghost, and began to speak with other tongues, as the Spirit gave them utterance" (Acts 2:1–4) (emphasis added).

Through the prophet Daniel, the Lord also revealed when Jesus would enter the last phase of His ministry for human salvation and when the sanctuary in heaven would be finally cleansed and justified:

"...How long shall be the vision concerning the daily sacrifice, and the transgression of desolation, to give both the sanctuary and the host to be trodden under foot? And he said unto me, *Unto two thousand and three hundred days*; then shall the sanctuary be cleansed" (Dan. 8:13, 14) (emphasis added).

Some of the times in God's plan are known only to God (see Acts 1:7). But the times that are revealed to us in His holy word are for us and are for our blessing.

"The secret things belong unto the LORD our God: but *those things which are revealed belong unto us and to our children for ever*, that we may do all the words of this law" (Deut. 29:29) (emphasis added).

The Times of Refreshing

It is also clearly revealed in the Scriptures that God will finish His work of salvation and bring the plan of redemption to its purposed glorious climax in a soon-coming dispensation of time.

"Repent ye therefore, and be converted, that your sins may be blotted out, *when the times of refreshing* shall come from the presence of the Lord. And he shall send Jesus Christ, which before was preached unto you: Whom the heaven must receive *until the times of restitution of all things*, which God hath spoken by the mouth of all his holy prophets since the world began" (Acts 3:19–21) (emphasis added).

Notice that, at the opening of the gospel of Jesus Christ, Peter, speaking by the Holy Ghost, points us to hope for the final realization of God's plan at its close: when the sanctuary in heaven should be cleansed by having the sins of God's people "blotted out." Indeed, there is a season or time when God will bring to glorious fulfillment the goals and purposes of the everlasting covenant and the previous Scripture reveals that these very things have been spoken by all of the holy prophets since the world began.

Should we not, therefore, seek to know the times that God has been pleased to reveal to us in the Scriptures, so that we may know what God has foretold concerning when He will accomplish the concluding steps of the plan of redemption?

We know that, in following Christ and being led by His Spirit, we shall be in the channel of blessing when the times should be accomplished. The best example of this is when the Holy Spirit was poured out at Pentecost. The disciples obeyed Christ's instruction to tarry in Jerusalem until the promised power would come upon them; but they didn't know it would come on the day of Pentecost (at least it has not been revealed that they knew; possibly they may have thought it might happen at that time).

> "There is a season or time when God will bring to glorious fulfillment the goals and purposes of the everlasting covenant."

But when it came to the close of the 2,300 days of Daniel 8:14, when the Angel (who is the Wonderful Numberer, see Dan. 8:13, KJV margin) said that the sanctuary would be cleansed, the Lord stirred up the hearts of faithful believers to study His Word; in various places around the world, at the same time, men came under conviction that the prophecy was soon to be fulfilled, and they proclaimed what they thought was the event to happen when the 2,300 days would end—the second coming of Christ. So again, led by the Holy Spirit, faithful men searched the Scriptures diligently to understand the time in which the events pointed to in the Scriptures would be fulfilled.

Can we know when *the times of refreshing and the times of restitution of all things* (see Acts 3:19, 21) shall be? Before considering the times that Peter, by the Holy Spirit, was referring to, let us first consider what happens at the times of refreshing and the times of restitution of all things.

"The times of restitution of all things" (Acts 3:21) (emphasis added) involves much, but maybe the simplest explanation is that it describes the time when God's people are restored, by the righteousness of Christ, to the sinless purity mankind had in the garden of Eden, before Adam's fall into sin which gave the dominion of this earth into the hands of Satan.

"And thou, O tower of the flock, the strong hold of the daughter of Zion, unto thee shall it come, even the *first dominion*; the kingdom shall come to the daughter of Jerusalem" (Mic. 4:8) (emphasis added).

Now what Peter calls ***"the times of refreshing"*** (Acts 3:19) (emphasis added) is closely connected to ***"the times of restitution"*** (Acts 3:21) (emphasis added) and is one of the necessary causes that brings it about.

In the Scripture of Acts 3:19, the ***"times of refreshing"*** is expressly stated to take place when the sins of God's people are "**blotted out**."

"Repent ye therefore, and be converted, that *your sins* may be *blotted out, when the times of refreshing shall come from the presence of the Lord*" (Acts 3:19) (emphasis added).

The Day of Atonement

The blotting out of the sins of God's people is a very specific event described in the Holy Scriptures. This is not referring to sins being forgiven but when all of the sins of God's people are completely erased from being recorded in the sanctuary. We find when this service takes place in the Old Testament in the book of Leviticus, which details for us the sanctuary service, where the gospel of the atonement of Jesus Christ for our sins is explained in the types and figures of the earthly sanctuary. These are God's instructors to teach us about what Christ would do in reality in the heavenly sanctuary (see Heb. 8:5; Heb. 9:24).

Leviticus chapter 16 describes the special service God instituted for the final cleansing of His sanctuary, where the sins of His people had accumulated all during the year of the typical ministration (as discussed in chapter 2). This special service to cleanse the sanctuary by blotting out the sins recorded there, took place on the Day of Atonement, which the Scriptures declare happens on the tenth day of the seventh month in God's sacred calendar.

"And this shall be a statute for ever unto you: that in the seventh month, on the tenth day of the month, ye shall afflict your souls, and do no work at all. whether it be one of your own country, or a stranger that sojourneth among you: For on that day shall the priest make an atonement for you, to cleanse you, that ye may be clean from all your sins before the LORD. It shall be a sabbath of rest unto you, and ye shall afflict your souls, by a statute for ever" (Lev. 16:29–31).

We have been discussing the message concerning Christ's atonement for our sins as provided for us in the everlasting covenant, to give us the perfect righteousness of Christ's Own eternal life. As we have been shown in the vision of Christ revealed to Habakkuk, the prophet, and made plain on the tables of the law of God — we see Christ as the fountain of the atonement: from Him pours out His sacred blood of sprinkling (see Heb. 12:24) which shall accomplish the cleansing of the heavenly sanctuary, where our sins are to be blotted out from being recorded there in God's house.

But it is not in the sanctuary in heaven alone that our sins need to be blotted out. Remember we are also shown in the vision of Christ, that from Jesus is shooting forth bright beams of light from His pierced side, representing that His Holy Spirit, which He sends into our hearts to cleanse us from sin, comes from His pierced side, from His heart, to make our hearts like His, pure and undefiled.

We have been receiving the Holy Spirit (also called in scripture "the divine nature" 2 Peter 1:4) in varying measures as believers in Christ, but the Scriptures point to a time when God's people are to be given an overwhelming endowment of the Spirit to complete the finishing work of cleansing our hearts from sin and sealing the living believers, who shall be privileged to see that day, to never sin again!

The Final Warning

The final outpouring of the Holy Spirit, which seals God's people, is also represented as preparing them to give the most powerful presentation of the gospel to the people of the world as has ever been given, to awaken a sleeping church, and to warn the wicked world before the wrath of God is poured out in the seven last plagues.

> **And after these things I saw another angel come down from heaven, having great power; and the earth was lightened with his glory.** ***And he cried mightily with a strong voice, saying, Babylon the great is fallen, is fallen*****, and is become the habitation of devils, and the hold of every foul spirit, and a cage of every unclean and hateful bird. For all nations have drunk of the wine of the wrath of her fornication, and the kings of the earth have committed fornication with her, and the merchants of the earth are waxed rich through the abundance of her delicacies.** ***And I heard another voice from heaven, saying, Come out of her, my people, that ye be not partakers of her sins, and that ye receive not of her plagues.*** (Rev. 18:1–4) (emphasis added)

This prophecy of the Angel coming down from heaven and lighting the earth with his glory is describing the time when the people of God receive the latter rain of God's Spirit to prepare them for the trying hour before them. The message and power of this Angel of Revelation 18:1, warning God's people to come out of Babylon, is a repetition and enlargement of the second angel's message of Revelation 14:8.

"And there followed another angel, saying, ***Babylon is fallen, is fallen*****, that great city, because she made all nations**

drink of the wine of the wrath of her fornication" (Rev. 14:8) (emphasis added).

The second angel's message of Revelation 14:8 is part of a three-fold message represented as being given by three angels **"flying in the midst of heaven,"** as found in Revelation 14:6–12.

God's last message of mercy to our world.
Revelation 14:6-12 and 18:1-4

These messages constitute the last warning message to the inhabitants of the world and are to prepare God's people for the great conflict they must meet in the last days.

> **And I saw another angel fly in the midst of heaven, having *the everlasting gospel* to preach unto them that dwell on the earth, and to every nation, and kindred, and tongue, and people, Saying with a loud voice, *Fear God*, and give glory to him; for the hour of his judgment is come: *and worship him* that made heaven, and earth, and the sea, and the fountains of waters.**
>
> **And there followed another angel, saying, Babylon is fallen, is fallen, that great city, because she made all nations drink of the wine of the wrath of her fornication.**
>
> **And the third angel followed them, saying with a loud voice, *If any man worship the beast and his image, and receive his mark in his forehead, or in his hand, The same shall drink of the wine of the wrath of God, which is poured out without mixture into the cup of his indignation*; and he shall be tormented with fire and brimstone in the presence of the holy angels, and in the presence of the Lamb: And the smoke of their torment ascendeth up for ever and ever: and they have no rest day nor night, who worship the beast and his image, and whosoever receiveth the mark of his name. *Here is the patience of the saints: here are they that keep the commandments of God, and the faith of Jesus*.** (Rev. 14:6-12) (emphasis added)

The first angel's message found in Revelation 14:6–7 declares the everlasting gospel to all nations and commands them to fear God and worship the Creator who has made all things.

The everlasting gospel brought to light here in the first angel's message is the end-time presentation of the gospel of Jesus—unfolding the present truth of the everlasting covenant of righteousness, as is being presented in this book.

When the first angel announces that **"the hour of His judgment is come"** (Rev. 14:7), this signifies that this message could not be preached until after Christ entered the Most Holy Place of the heavenly sanctuary, which took place on October 22, 1844 (this is in reference to the date for when the 2300 days of Daniel 8:14 should be fulfilled, when it was announced that the sanctuary would be cleansed). While Christ is making the final atonement in the Holiest of all, He also judges who among His professed followers truly repented of their sins and shall have a place with Him eternally in His kingdom. Everyone who has ever professed faith in Christ and confessed their sins, beginning with Adam after his fall, down to the present time until the sanctuary is closed, is included in this judgment (see Rev. 14:7). This final cleansing of the sanctuary and judging of His people also, in many aspects, represents that 'the time of *the judgment of Him* has come'— this is because the closing of the great controversy between Christ and Satan involves how Christ's professed followers 'judge' our Lord Jesus and the character of the living God, as the record books of our thoughts and actions in heaven accurately reveal if we truly believe our Lord and His Word (see Dan. 7:10; Luke 19:11–27).

The second angel's message, which is also proclaimed with great power by the angel of Revelation 18:1, declares that the apostate system of false Christianity called *Babylon* is fallen and warns that God's people must separate themselves from communion with her, lest they be partakers of her fornications (her spiritual adultery against God) and thereby receive also of her plagues (see Rev. 14:8; Rev. 18:2–4).

Then the third angel's message brings to view a terrible conflict and warns every living soul upon the earth not to receive the mark of the beast (the details of which are in Revelation chapter 13). If anyone receives the mark of the beast, God threatens the most terrible punishment ever recorded in the Bible: the wrath of God unmingled with mercy! The third angel's message ends by revealing the people who will receive salvation in this final conflict, which shall end in the seven last plagues.

"Here is the patience of the saints: here are they that keep the commandments of God, and the faith of Jesus" (Rev. 14:12).

Preparing for the Final Conflict

The reality that the Scriptures are opening before us, especially in the last book of the Bible with the words **"the Revelation of Jesus Christ"** (Rev. 1:1), tells us that we are to prepare our hearts and minds to receive by saving faith the finishing of Christ's work in the everlasting covenant; He promises to fill us with the righteousness of God (see Rev. 19:8, Rev. 10:7, Eze. 36:25-28). At the same time we are shown that we shall be brought into one great final conflict with Satan and the powers of earth.

See it here, as described in the book of Daniel, which is a parallel prophetic book to the book of Revelation.

> **And at that time shall Michael stand up, the great prince which standeth for the children of thy people: and there shall be a *time of trouble*, such as never was since there was a nation even to that same time: and at that time thy people shall be delivered, every one that shall be found written in the book. And many of them that sleep in the dust of the earth shall awake, some to everlasting life, and some to shame and everlasting contempt. And they that be wise shall shine as the brightness of the firmament; *and they that turn many to righteousness as the stars for ever and ever*.** (Dan. 12:1–3) (emphasis added)

In the last days as the winds of strife are ready to be released (see Rev. 7:1–3), the devil will be permitted to plunge the earth into one final cataclysm, called in Scripture "***a time of trouble, such as never was…***" (Dan. 12:1, NKJV) (emphasis added).

Satan does this because he sees that not only are people being sealed in God's righteousness but these same ones also shall **"...turn many to righteousness..."** (Dan. 12:3). So the Devil goes forth and influences the inhabitants of the earth whom he has control over—those who have received the mark of the beast—to totally commit to destroying God's people, those who are the end-time Israel of God, keeping (honoring) God's commandments.

"And the dragon was wroth with the woman, and went to make war *with the remnant of her seed, which keep the commandments of God, and have the testimony of Jesus Christ*" (Rev. 12:17) (emphasis added).

In this present message, we have been shown the vision of Christ, as seen by the prophet Habakkuk, made plain upon the tables of God's law, which has been lifted up as an ensign, a standard or banner, calling all who hear, understand, and believe to **"look at it and live"** (Num. 21:8, NIV) and rally to the ensign, which is "**The LORD our righteousness**" (Jer. 23:6).

The purpose of the message is to reveal Christ and His present truth revelations of Himself: He is the fountain from whence our atonement flows—the blood of sprinkling and His Holy Spirit, the Soul of His life. This message is also meant to call God's people to gather to Christ—to come out of the wicked world and prepare for the conflict before them—by revealing these truths of Jesus made plain upon the tables. Those who stand under the ensign of the righteousness of God become God's purpose and goal in these last days before Jesus returns: they are the end-time Israel of God, who represent the "mystery of God finished."

"But *in the days of the voice of the seventh angel*, when he shall begin to sound, *the mystery of God should be finished*, as he hath declared to his servants the prophets" (Rev. 10:7) (emphasis added).

This triumph of God's people is in the last days when the Israel of God finally gets the victory over the devil and the mark of the beast; this has been the long-looked-for climax of the plan of redemption and what the prophets and holy, faithful men of past ages have longed for.

This is the great hope of righteousness by faith (see Gal. 5:5) in Christ's atonement which shall be accomplished at the end of time— ***"when the times of refreshing shall come from the presence of the Lord"*** (Acts 3:19) (emphasis added)—and this same time is also called ***"the days of the voice of the seventh angel, when he shall begin to sound"*** (Rev. 10:7) (emphasis added). The Scriptures reveal to us what is spoken by the voice of the seventh angel when he shall sound.

> **And the seventh angel sounded; and there were great voices in heaven, saying, *The kingdoms of this world are become the kingdoms of our Lord, and of his Christ*; and he shall reign for ever and ever. And the four and twenty elders, which sat before God on their seats, fell upon their faces, and worshipped God, Saying, We give thee thanks, O LORD God Almighty, which art, and wast, and art to come; because thou hast taken to thee thy great power, and hast reigned. And the nations were angry, and thy wrath is come, and the time of the dead, that they should be judged, and that thou shouldest give reward unto thy servants the prophets, and to the saints, and them that fear thy name, small and great; and shouldest destroy them which destroy the earth. *And the temple of God was opened in heaven, and there was seen in his temple the ark of his testament*: and there were lightnings, and voices, and thunderings, and an earthquake, and great hail.** (Rev. 11:15–19) (emphasis added)

The Times of the Covenant

Today, all to whom this message has come have a great opportunity to cooperate with God to finish the conflict, to bring this scene of misery to an end and anoint Jesus King and Lord of all. We are to cooperate with God **"...to make an end of sins ... and to bring in everlasting righteousness ...** ***and to anoint the most Holy*"** (Dan. 9:24) (emphasis added). The way this is accomplished is by accepting the great gift of the everlasting covenant — the righteousness of God. We must also understand a very important feature of the final conflict with Satan: the issue of worship and God's sacred times of worship.

In God's covenant, He has given to His people laws and statutes for their good always and to guard against wicked apostasy (see Deut. 6:24). Since the reformation that brought Christianity out of the Dark Ages, when many truths were lost in the general apostasy of the Christian church, God has been restoring those truths that were lost, one by one. When the 2300 days of Daniel 8:14 ended, Jesus entered the Most Holy Place of the heavenly sanctuary to begin His finishing work of the antitypical (the true) Day of Atonement in heaven; this happened in AD 1844. At that same time, God opened to His people on earth the truth of the heavenly sanctuary and also the importance of His people keeping the Ten Commandments, as they were seen to be in the ark of His covenant, in the Most Holy Place of the heavenly temple (see Rev. 11:19).

At that time, most Christians understood that they should keep and honor God's Ten Commandments (see Exod. 20:2–17). But they had generally stopped obeying the fourth commandment to rest on God's seventh-day Sabbath (from Friday evening at sunset to Saturday evening at sunset (see Gen. 1:31; Gen. 2:1–3) and to keep the Sabbath as set apart and holy because that in six days the Lord made the heaven and the earth then rested the seventh day and hallowed it (see the fourth commandment, Exod. 20:8–11).

The seventh-day Sabbath, which points to Yahuwah our Elohim as the Creator of the heavens and the earth, distinguishes the Lord as the true God from all false gods (see Jer. 10:11). The Sabbath is commanded by the Lord of Heaven to be remembered and observed as the memorial of the Creator's work (see Heb. 4:9, 10). All who keep the seventh day signify by this act that they are worshipers of Jehovah (Yahuwah, Hebrew transliteration). Thus the Sabbath is given as a sign of man's allegiance to His Creator and as a memorial to aid man in remembering that it is Christ who sanctifies him (see Exod. 31:13).

> "*The seventh-day Sabbath, which points to Yahuwah our Elohim as the Creator of the heavens and the earth, distinguishes the Lord as the true God from all false gods.*"

When the temple of God was opened after the 2300 days of Daniel 8:14 had finished and the ark of the covenant (which contain the Ten Commandments) was seen (see Rev. 11:19), the believers recommitted to honoring God's law, including the seventh-day Sabbath. This period of time witnessed the beginning of the Christian church recovering not only the laws of God's kingdom but also the times of the kingdom.

God's everlasting covenant is a covenant of faith; we are saved by believing in God's provision for us. Yet faith does not make void the necessity of obeying God's instructions He has given us.

Maybe the best example of this is the snake on the pole that Moses lifted up in the wilderness, as discussed in Chapter One. The healing that God gave when the Israelites looked to the snake on the pole was brought to them by their faith in the remedy He had provided, but they were required to demonstrate their faith by obeying God's spoken way, which was **"to look at it and live"** (Num. 21:8, NIV). It is the same with His laws and the times of the covenant today; they are all about drawing us closer to Christ, who is our salvation. We believe and obey His spoken instructions to honor our Creator and Redeemer and so that God may be glorified in our deliverance — for the righteousness of God cannot cover us while in rebellion and disregard of His Covenant.

The seventh-day Sabbath, being embedded in the heart of the Decalogue of God's Ten Commandments, which He wrote in stone when He came down upon Mount Sinai (see Exod. 19:11), is the standard or ensign not only of God's law, by faith in His word, but more especially of the times of His covenant.

"Moreover also I gave them my sabbaths, to be an [*ensign*] between me and them, that they might know that I am the LORD that makes them holy" (see Ezek. 20:12, 20) (emphasis added).

But the seventh-day Sabbath is not the only times of the Covenant that we are to receive by faith as we accept the everlasting covenant (remember times and the covenant are connected, see Isa. 56:4, 6). God's sacred calendar of times and festivals are revealed in the everlasting covenant law of God as well.

"And the LORD spake unto Moses, saying, Speak unto the children of Israel, and say unto them, *Concerning the feasts of the LORD, which ye shall proclaim to be holy convocations, even these are my feasts*. Six days shall work be done: but the seventh day is the sabbath of rest, an holy convocation; ye shall do no work therein: it is the sabbath of the LORD in all your dwellings. These are the feasts of the LORD, even holy convocations, which ye shall proclaim in their seasons" (Lev. 23: 1–4) (emphasis added).

The Scriptures of Leviticus chapter 23 list the sacred appointed worship times of the Lord: the seventh-day Sabbath (Lev. 23:3), the Passover and Feast of Unleavened Bread (Lev. 23:5–8), Firstfruits (Lev. 23:10–21), The solemnity of blowing of Trumpets (Lev. 23:24, 25), the Day of Atonement (Lev. 23:27–33) and the Feast of Tabernacles (Lev. 23:34–36).

The Wicked Plan to Change God's Law

Today, most of the Christian churches do not honor and are not even aware of when these appointed times of worshiping the King occur. Because of this, these times of refreshing from the presence of the Lord pass over God's people unawares. To receive the blessings God intends for us, we must take hold of them by active faith. God's people being unmindful of His sacred worship times, and many even outright rejecting them, is just as the devil would have it to be.

But even more than that, the devil has used mystery Babylon, the apostate fallen church which claims to be Christian, to teach His people that these sacred times have been abolished; then he has given false times of worship in their place. The change or abolishing of the law of God was foretold in the Scriptures.

"And he shall speak great words against the most High, and shall wear out the saints of the most High, *and think to change times and laws*: and they shall be given into his hand until a time and times and the dividing of time" (Dan. 7:25) (emphasis added).

The entity which speaks great words against God and attempts to change His law, as spoken of in the Scripture quoted previously is **"...Babylon the great,"** as she is identified in Revelation 17:5, but this is also the same blasphemous **"little horn"** of Daniel 7:8, 25. Therefore God has revealed that He will cause His end-time Israel to preach the everlasting gospel message, which is to be given with the increased power of the angel of Revelation 18:1, declaring that Babylon the great has fallen through her apostasy against God's plainest teachings and instructions. As a result, God urgently calls His people to depart from the midst of her, so they be not partakers of her sins, which would cause them to receive of her plagues (see Jer. 51:6; Rev. 18:1–4).

Babylon the great apostatized from the true biblical faith and decreed a change in God's law during the Dark Ages; this was done by forsaking the word of God and accepting the practices of the world and compromising with worldly governments. Mystery Babylon is the fallen Roman church of the papal system. In the Dark Ages she decreed that Christians should no longer honor God's seventh-day Sabbath and she replaced the Sabbath with the first day of the week, which is so named as *Sunday*, the day of the Sun. But the Sabbath was not the only time which the apostate Roman church abolished; she also claimed the authority to change all of God's appointed worship times in God's sacred calendar (as discussed in Leviticus 23) and replace them with pagan times.

The Scriptures reveal that it was Satan himself, also called in scripture *"the dragon"* (see Rev. 12:9), who gave the apostate Roman church the evil power to conspire to rule Christianity worldwide and attempt to change God's covenant times and laws, to the intent that the people who are thus deceived should reject Christ and not be saved.

Ultimately, the deceitful ways of the Roman Catholic Church, which she developed during the Dark Ages, will lead to the final crisis in earth's history, as described in the book of Revelation chapter 13, and it will involve other fallen Christian churches influencing their state and national governments to make an "image to the beast" by following the ways and example of the fallen mother church of Rome:

> **And I stood upon the sand of the sea, and saw a beast rise up out of the sea, having seven heads and ten horns, and upon his horns ten crowns, and upon his heads the name of blasphemy. And the beast which I saw was like unto a leopard, and his feet were as the feet of a bear, and his mouth as the mouth of a lion: and the dragon gave him his power, and his seat, and great authority. And I saw one of his heads as it were wounded to death; and his deadly wound was healed: and all the world wondered after the beast. *And they worshipped the dragon which gave power unto the beast: and they worshipped the beast, saying, Who is like unto the beast? who is able to make war with him?* And there was given unto him a mouth speaking great things and blasphemies;**

> **and power was given unto him to continue forty and two months. And he opened his mouth in blasphemy against God, to blaspheme his name, and his tabernacle, and them that dwell in heaven. And it was given unto him to make war with the saints, and to overcome them: and power was given him over all kindreds, and tongues, and nations.** ***And all that dwell upon the earth shall worship him, whose names are not written in the book of life of the Lamb slain from the foundation of the world.*** **. . . And I beheld another beast coming up out of the earth; and he had two horns like a lamb, and he spake as a dragon. And he exerciseth all the power of the first beast before him, and causeth the earth and them which dwell therein to worship the first beast, whose deadly wound was healed. And he doeth great wonders, so that he maketh fire come down from heaven on the earth in the sight of men, And deceiveth them that dwell on the earth by the means of those miracles which he had power to do in the sight of the beast; saying to them that dwell on the earth, that they should make an image to the beast, which had the wound by a sword, and did live. And he had power to give life unto the image of the beast, that the image of the beast should both speak, and cause that as many as would not worship the image of the beast should be killed.** (Rev. 13:1-8, 11-15) (emphasis added)

The devil and his representative system on the earth is called in the Scriptures "the beast" (see Rev. 17:11; Rev. 13:1–4) and "**MYSTERY, BABYLON THE GREAT, THE MOTHER OF HARLOTS AND ABOMINATIONS OF THE EARTH**" (Rev. 17:5) (emphasis added). The Roman church became the fallen mystery Babylon, Mother of harlots and abominations when it rejected faith in God's word and thereby no longer sought to gain true righteousness from God.

Therefore, she sought to connect herself with governmental power, called in Scriptures "***the kings of the earth***" (Rev. 17:2), to enforce her dogmas. Since she turned away from God's power, the inevitable result was that she formed a combination of church and state power, which is apostasy against true faith in Jesus' power; the Scriptures call this combining of church with state power *'fornication'* with the kings of the earth (see Rev. 17:2; Rev. 18:3, 9). When other churches do as this mother harlot has done and make a church and state connection to enforce their dogmas, they become fallen daughters of the mother harlot church and they are making an ***"image to the beast"*** (Rev. 13:14) (emphasis added).

The dreadful mark of the beast crisis, foreshadowed in the book of Revelation, is introduced in close connection with "**the image of the beast**" (Rev. 13:15–17). The agent of this tyranny is the second beast of Revelation (see Rev. 13:11–14). There have been many interpretations of these Scriptures over the years as to what the mark of the beast is, but it is clear that the second beast will do the same as the first beast, which is identified as the fallen church of Rome. The second beast will essentially replicate the tyranny which the church of Rome

They shall make an image to the beast.

has done in the past (during the Dark Ages). That is why it is called an "image to the beast."

The beast, the fallen church of Rome, attempted to change God's law and the times of His covenant (see Dan 7:25). She then proceeded to persecute anyone who dared disagree with her teachings to the extent that she would put to death Christians who remained steadfast to worship God according to the Scriptures in defiance of the decrees by which the church of Rome tried to change God's worship times and laws (see Rev. 13:7). Those whose consciences were bound to the word of God and those who decided to continue to honor God's seventh-day Sabbath (and not honor the first day of the week called *Sunday,* which the apostate church decreed all Christians must honor) were pursued by the church of Rome with deadly cruelty. She did these things by influencing and controlling the governing powers of countries under her sway to use state power to punish those who defied her attempts to control the conscience of individuals. The wisdom and power of love to convince the consciences of men is the work of God alone; therefore, all attempts of men in church leadership to try to force the consciences of their fellow men through sanctions and torture is satanic cruelty and apostasy against the God they claim to serve. This is what will be repeated when the second beast of Revelation 13 makes an "**image to the beast**" and, in doing this, the second beast will cause all to worship the first beast, the church of Rome, by forcing people to honor its dogmas and decrees and ultimately to receiving the mark of the beast (see Rev. 13:11–16). The mark of the beast is a symbol of the apostate church's assumed power to change God's times and laws.

During the Dark Ages, the Roman church attempted to force all people to obey its religious decrees and participate in worship, if need be, against their will; this is always anti-Christian and not of God. The Bible warns us of the great calamity that will result when the churches influence the government to repeat this same work of the antichrist (see Rev. 13:15). Thereupon, any decree in these last days by the government of a country, to enforce by state power, and influenced by fallen, apostate Christian churches, to mandate and compel people to participate in so-called "Christian" worship, such as Sunday worship, will be the fulfillment of the dreaded "***mark* of the beast**." This is Babylon's mark, the sign of her claim to possess the power to change God's law, and Christians for too long have agreed that she had the power to change the seventh-day Sabbath to the first day of the week called Sunday (which has no authority in God's Word to have replaced God's seventh-day Sabbath).

Satan is the true instigator who caused the fallen church of Rome, this Babylon the great, to seek to change God's law. The fallen angel Lucifer is trying to prevent God's people from receiving the final atonement and being cleansed from sin and sealed by receiving the long-looked-for great outpouring of God's Spirit to fill them with the power to overcome the devil in the last great conflict that is soon to come.

Satan, working through the apostate church, is trying to abolish **"the times of refreshing"** (Acts 3:19), when God's people will finally grow up into Christ (see Eph. 4:15) by being filled with the righteousness of God that will defeat the devil while he still has power to reign on earth. This demonstration of God's character in an entire group of righteous individuals—the end-time Israel of God—will bring to an end this long-standing controversy over the government and character of God that Satan started in heaven, which has continued upon this earth.

Before he was banished from the courts of heaven, Lucifer told the angels that he had a better system of government than God and Jesus Christ (see Isa. 14:13, 14). The angels, having no knowledge of evil, could not clearly comprehend the results of Satan's rebellion; so God has given Satan many centuries of opportunity upon the earth to develop the working out of his character, ideas, and his rulership in contrast to God's ways, which have also been manifest in our world (see Rev. 12:12, 13; Job 2:1–10).

Christ revealed the true character of God in His victorious life upon the earth and corrected the false views of God that Satan had led mankind to believe (John 17:4). But the devil, after being defeated at the cross of Calvary, then refocused his efforts and charged that most of Jesus' professed followers, in fact, were obeying Satan, the prince of this world, and not Christ the Lamb of God (see Rom. 6:16; 2 Thess. 2:3–12; 2 Cor. 11:13–15). Therefore, God has shown us in His Holy Word that, at the end of time, Satan's accusations against God will finally be answered and silenced when God has His end-time group of righteous individuals of Israel (see Dan. 8:13,14; Heb. 10:16–18; Ezek. 36:21–38). Once sealed in His righteousness, each person will not dishonor Christ even though the devil will try everything possible to get even just one of them to sin, but he will not succeed (see Rev. 14:1–4).

This is the conflict we are to prepare for by accepting the present truth that is now shining. We are to joyfully accept God's ways and instructions for our good, so that we receive all the blessings and power He has promised in His covenant. (He has so many "***exceeding great and precious promises***" for us (see 2 Peter 1:4)! God the Father and Christ the Lamb will be glorified in the demonstration of the Israel of God at the end of time:

"Whereby are given unto us exceeding great and precious promises: that by these ye might be partakers of the divine nature, having escaped the corruption that is in the world through lust" (2 Peter 1:4).

"Here is the patience of the saints: here are they that keep the commandments of God, and the faith of Jesus" (Rev. 14:12).

"The God of peace will soon crush Satan under your feet. The grace of our Lord Jesus Christ be with you" (Rom. 16:20, NIV).

And these overcomers (which is what the name *Israel* means) will be blessed forever in the victory they gained by faith in God and in the Lamb.

> **And I saw as it were a sea of glass mingled with fire: and *them that had gotten the victory over the beast, and over his image, and over his mark, and over the number of his name,* stand on the sea of glass, having the harps of God. And they sing the song of Moses the servant of God, and the song of the Lamb, saying, Great and marvellous are thy works, Lord God Almighty; just and true are thy ways, thou King of saints. Who shall not fear thee, O Lord, and glorify thy name? for thou only art holy: for all nations shall come and worship before thee; for thy judgments are made manifest.** (Rev. 15:2–4) (emphasis added)

One Final Offering

We are now living in the time of the antitypical Day of Atonement. This is brought to view in the Scriptures of Daniel chapter 8 where Christ Himself, the Wonderful Numberer, tells His people when the sanctuary in heaven shall be cleansed, at the end of the 2300 days (see Dan. 8:13, 14, KJV margin).

The 2300 days ended in 1844 and Jesus entered the Most Holy Place of the heavenly sanctuary on the Day of Atonement (Yom Kippur) of that year, which was on October 22, 1844.

Jesus will complete His final work in the sanctuary above and sprinkle His sacred blood on the mercy seat one final time on a Day of Atonement in a soon coming year. It behooves us to restore the Bible teachings of God's covenant, which includes His sacred times of worship and atonement, so that we may be looking unto Jesus and, by faith, honor His Word, the Bible, which He has given to us to help us in receiving all He has promised.

If the churches had not been so quick to agree with the fallen Roman church and attempt to abolish the law of God, many more would have discerned that Jesus said that not one jot or tittle of His law will pass away until all be fulfilled (see Matt. 5:17, 18), and we can plainly see that not yet has everything been fulfilled that was typified in the ceremonial law.

During the services on the Day of Atonement, as described in Leviticus 16, the High Priest goes into the Most Holy Place with the blood of a special offering which had not been made during the entire sacred year.

On the Day of Atonement, two goats are taken as a sin offering from the people of the congregation, and the High Priest cast lots to determine which goat should be the Lord's goat and which one shall be Azazel, the scapegoat (see Lev. 16:5, 7–10, 15, 16). The Lord's goat was then slain and his blood brought into the Most Holy Place to sprinkle seven times on the mercy seat, which rested on top of the ark of the covenant (see Lev. 16:14–16). Then the High Priest was to leave the Most Holy Place and confess all of the sins of the children of Israel over the head of the scapegoat; then the scapegoat was led away out of the camp of Israel never to return, bearing the sins of all the people (see Lev. 16:21, 22).

"*If the churches had not been so quick to agree with the fallen Roman church and attempt to abolish the law of God, many more would have discerned that Jesus said that not one jot or tittle of His law will pass away until all be fulfilled.*"

This typical service represented when Christ, our great High Priest, will blot out the sins of His people at the close of the antitypical Day of Atonement. The scapegoat represents Satan, who is the originator of sin and will finally have the sins of God's people returned upon his own head (which is why he has worked so hard through the apostate church to try to hide this truth from God's people).

But there is something very special about the offering of the Lord's goat that should occupy our attention at this time. All during the sacred year of God's calendar, as offerings were brought to the sanctuary, sins were confessed over them and the animals were slain and then their blood was brought into the sanctuary, transferring the sins of God's people to the sanctuary (as discussed in Chapter Two). This is what made it necessary for the Lord to institute the special services of the Day of Atonement when God's house would be cleansed of the sins that had been accumulating there all year. Even on the Day of Atonement sins are still being transferred to the sanctuary through the blood of the bullock offered for the house of the High Priest (see Lev. 16:3, 6, 11–14; Heb. 3:6). But the offering of the Lord's goat is very special and nothing like this offering ever took place during God's sacred calendar year. Therefore, the reality of this Offering has never taken place in the heavenly sanctuary, because in Leviticus 16 this offering of the Lord's goat is the final sacrifice that cleanses the sanctuary.

What makes the offering of the Lord's goat so special is not the animal, for goats were offered all through the sacred year. What makes this offering so special is that no sins were confessed over the Lord's goat before it was slain and its blood brought into the sanctuary.[v]

The purpose of the blood of the Lord's goat is not to transfer sins to the sanctuary as other sacrifices, but its blood is to cleanse the sins recorded there in the sanctuary and to blot them out forever; its blood is sprinkled seven times over the mercy seat and the sanctuary is cleansed (see Lev. 16:14, 15). This is ***"the blood of the everlasting covenant"*** (Heb. 13:20, 21) (emphasis added) which makes God's people perfect! Until the Day of Atonement comes, no service like this takes place during the sacred year, and the reality of this Offering has not yet taken place in heaven. This is the final atonement, witnessed to in the law of God, which will bring about the long-looked-for blotting out of sins from the heavenly sanctuary and from the hearts of God's people! Jesus, on a Day of Atonement very soon, will sprinkle His sacred blood one final time, not to transfer fresh sins to the sanctuary, but to cleanse the sanctuary in heaven forever. When Jesus will sprinkle His sacred blood that final time upon the mercy seat, in fulfillment of the reality of the offering of the Lord's goat on a Day of Atonement in God's calendar one year very soon, at that same time He will send forth the great outpouring of His Holy Spirit into the hearts of His believers to seal them. From that day, the Israel of God will never sin again:

"In those days, and in that time, saith the Lord, the iniquity of Israel shall be sought for, and there shall be none; and the sins of Judah, and they not be found…" (Jer. 50:20)

"Repent ye therefore, and be converted, that your sins may be blotted out, when the times of refreshing shall come from the presence of the Lord" (Acts 3:19).

"In those days shall Judah be saved, and Jerusalem shall dwell safely: *and this is the name wherewith she shall be called, The LORD our righteousness*" (Jer. 33:16) (emphasis added).

The Gathering Time of the Israel of God

The saints of God are soon to be brought into close conflict with "**the image of the beast**"—those fallen apostate churches and government powers, who the churches will gain influence over, in an unlawful alliance to persecute God's true church. These who have rejected the righteousness of God and have agreed with Rome in her attempt to abolish God's law and the times of His covenant, thereby becoming mystery Babylon's daughters, will play their part to fulfill the prophecy of Revelation 13.

According to the Scriptures, they will **"make an image to the beast"** (Rev. 13:14) and try to compel everyone to receive the mark of the beast in their forehead or their right hand.

"And he had power to give life unto the image of the beast, that the image of the beast should both speak, and cause that as many as would not worship the image of the beast should be killed. **And he causeth all, both small and great, rich and poor, free and bond, to receive a mark in their right hand, or in their foreheads:** ***And that no man might buy or sell, save he that had the mark,*** **or the name of the beast, or the number of his name"** (Rev. 13:15–17) (emphasis added).

It is the work of that angel of Revelation 18:1, who is a representation of Christ coming to His people as the great outpouring of His Holy Spirit "**when the times of refreshing shall come from the presence of the Lord**" (Acts 3:19) to seal the Israel of God and fill them with the great power of God to give the final warning to the whole world. On the Day of Atonement, the blood of the Lord's goat was sprinkled seven times over the mercy seat (see Lev. 16:14, 15); this represents not only the completeness of the cleansing to be accomplished, but also how the final warning will swell in power as the people of God receive the latter rain of Christ's Spirit unto fullness. Perhaps the message of warning will swell over a seven-year period of time as well. God is faithful; this latter rain power of Christ's Spirit is given so that all who hear God's message will be warned that they must come out of the fallen churches before probation is closed and the wrath of God is poured out upon those who reject God's mercy and His righteousness.

> **And after these things I saw another angel come down from heaven, having great power; and the earth was lightened with his glory. And he cried mightily with a strong voice, saying, Babylon the great is fallen, is fallen, and is become the habitation of devils, and the hold of every foul spirit, and a cage of every unclean and hateful bird. For all nations have drunk of the wine of the wrath of her fornication, and the kings of the earth have committed**

> **fornication with her, and the merchants of the earth are waxed rich through the abundance of her delicacies. And I heard another voice from heaven, saying, *Come out of her, my people, that ye be not partakers of her sins, and that ye receive not of her plagues*. For her sins have reached unto heaven, and God hath remembered her iniquities.** (Rev. 18:1–4) (emphasis added)

These wonderful events that are the climatic scenes to take place in the finishing work of the plan of redemption are clearly taught in God's sacred appointed times in His calendar. Satan has diligently worked to hide these things from the minds of the people of God, but God is calling upon us to revive His sacred calendar of worship times as they are still ordained to minister to us in showing us the times in God's schedule. Even the wonderful Feast of Tabernacles, which is typical of Christ's second coming and represents when God will dwell, or tabernacle, with His people, has yet to be fulfilled.

"And I heard a great voice out of heaven saying, Behold, *the tabernacle of God is with men, and he will dwell with them*, and they shall be his people, and God himself shall be with them, and be their God" (Rev. 21:3) (emphasis added).

"For verily I say unto you, Till heaven and earth pass, one jot or one tittle shall in no wise pass from the law, till all be fulfilled" (Matt. 5:18).

The symbolic types of the Scriptures certainly do not pass away before they are even fulfilled, and actually there is much evidence that God's sacred calendar will endure even in eternity (see Isa. 66:22, 23; Luke 22:15, 16). What is more, we should consider the great blessings that God has for us in receiving, by faith in His Word, the instructions He has given those who know and trust Him, to bless us. The Feast of Tabernacles is predominantly a celebration of being cleansed from sin and sealed in God's love as it comes shortly after the Day of Atonement in God's calendar. It is a time for the people of God to gather in great thankfulness to God for the blessings He has bountifully bestowed and to encourage and strengthen one another. Well would it be for the people of God to keep these sacred festivals of God's statutes in remembrance until Christ shall come and receive His bride, His church, unto Himself (see Mal. 4:4–6, Eph. 5:27).

God is calling on us to revive the understanding in the Christian dispensation that He has a holy schedule of blessings. With this knowledge we may then watch and know when the seventh month comes during each year so that, *especially in the solemnity of the Day of Atonement, we may gather (physically and spiritually) to afflict our souls* (see Lev. 16:29–31) *and to corporately pray for Jesus to offer the last offering of His blood*, typified by the offering of the Lord's goat, so that He may cleanse the sanctuary and our hearts to prepare us for the trying hour before us. This is represented in Scripture as God's people offering to Him a truly righteous offering by faith.

"But who may abide the day of his coming? and who shall stand when he appeareth? for he is like a refiner's fire, and like fullers' soap: And he shall sit as a refiner and purifier of silver: and he shall purify the sons of Levi, and purge them as gold and silver, *that they may offer unto the LORD an offering in righteousness*" (Mal. 3:2, 3) (emphasis added).

This Scripture is describing the work of Jesus, our Lamb offering and Great High Priest in heaven. He is working, even now through this message, to purify us to become the end-time Israel of God, that we may corporately offer to God the blood of Jesus by faith, to bring to an end this scene of misery on earth. This is the focus and climax of this message brought to you in this book: the purpose is to make ready a people prepared to meet our Lord when He shall return.

"Gather my saints together unto me; those that have made a covenant with me by sacrifice" (Ps. 50:5).

These things are all inherent in the vision of Christ made plain upon the tables of God's law. As mentioned, the blood of

Christ's sacrifice, made plain upon the second table of God's law represents "Love to Man." His blood is still shed for the forgiveness of our sins and, on a Day of Atonement one year very soon, it will be shed not to transfer sins but to finally cleanse the heavenly sanctuary.

We have also discussed the bright beams shining from Christ's pierced side, made plain upon the first table of God's law as "Love to God." How the light represents Christ's Holy Spirit, His eternal Life, which He sheds abroad in our hearts to cleanse us from sin and seal His people in His character at the same time He is cleansing the sanctuary in heaven from the defilement of our sins.

This chapter has presented the sacred appointed worship times of the everlasting covenant and the controversy Satan has instigated over God's sacred times. The times of the covenant are made plain upon the tables of God's law (in the fourth Commandment) as well as in the vision of Habakkuk ("**beside the sabbaths of the LORD**" (Lev. 23:38).

Behold upon the second table "Love to Man," where Christ is crucified upon the Cross, when the fountain of His sacred blood was first opened, when His heart was pierced by the cruel Roman spear—all of this took place on *the sacred time of the Passover* in God's calendar. This is the chief appointed time of the spring feasts.

Now behold, upon the first table where Christ is portrayed, no longer shedding His sacred blood, but now with bright beams of light shining from His same pierced side, in the glorious splendor of His second coming! The vision represents *the result of the sacred solemnity of the Day of Atonement*, when Christ is crowned King of kings and He shall close His sanctuary ministry in heaven because He will cleanse the heavenly temple on the Day of Atonement of some year very soon to come. This climactic event, bringing to an end the long standing Great Controversy in righteousness, is a mighty display of true "Love to God" - in which we play an integral part. The Day of Atonement is the most important appointed time of the year on God's calendar (called "the Sabbath of Sabbaths" in Hebrew [see Lev. 16:31]) and is the chief solemnity of the fall feasts.

"For the vision is yet for *an appointed time* (mo'ed - hebrew meaning: God's special festival), but at the end it shall speak and not lie..." (Hab. 2:3).

"The LORD is in his holy temple: let all the earth keep silence before him" (Hab. 2:20).

We are now lifting up the vision of Habakkuk which was to be made plain upon the tables of God's law. It is being lifted up as an ensign or a standard so that all may **"look at it and live"** (Num. 21:8, NIV) and receive the gift of the righteousness of God!

The Vision made plain upon the tables is to us as when Moses lifted the snake on a pole in the wilderness for the people of Israel who had been bitten by fiery serpents. They knew that the poison of the snake venom would end their lives quickly if God did not provide a remedy. As then, so it is now: the remedy to the deadly work of sin has been set before all who will read, understand, and believe (see Hab. 2:2–4). *It is as simple as believing God's message for us to be saved and, by faith, cooperating with God by accepting His provision and His instructions for our good always.*

What are those instructions that we are to receive by faith? Even the same as has been presented here: believe that Christ has sent this special message as bright beams of light shining from His pierced side, which is His life and character in a vision to be made plain upon the tables of God's law, representing the righteousness of God promised to us in the everlasting covenant. *We must believe in the complete atonement of Christ as revealed in the Vision made plain upon the tables*: His sacred blood, shed in heaven to cleanse our sins from the heavenly sanctuary, and His Holy Spirit sent to us as the Soul of the Life of Christ to cleanse our hearts and impress His character upon the hearts and minds of His church as the Spirit of sacrifice.[vi]

We must cease to believe and teach others that God has abolished His law, but instead see and understand, by receiving His divine illumination, that Christ is fulfilling the law of God in heaven and He imparts His righteousness to His church to show forth upon the earth His character, of which the law is a transcript. By receiving this message and "…**the hope of righteousness by faith**" (Gal. 5:5), we will learn to know when the seventh month comes and we will pray that Christ would offer the final offering in heaven. That final offering is the sprinkling of His blood upon the mercy seat represented by the Lord's goat of Leviticus 16—not to transfer sins to the sanctuary any longer (for we have confessed our sins and by God's grace and revelation put away our sinful practices)—but to blot out our sins which are recorded in the heavenly sanctuary and we wait for **"…the hope of righteousness by faith"** (Gal 5:5): the mighty outpouring of latter rain of Christ's Holy Spirit without measure.[vii]

When we accept the present truth of the everlasting gospel, and we gather and pray for Christ's "…**blood of sprinkling…**" (Heb. 12:24) to be offered in heaven (especially on the Day of Atonement), we do enter into the Most Holy Place of the heavenly sanctuary by faith. There we stand at the pierced side of our heavenly Bridegroom, who shall soon cleanse and purify His bride, preparatory to receiving her unto Himself (see Eph. 5:25–27) when He shall soon return in His glorious second coming. In the book of Revelation, the marriage represents the union of divinity with humanity. We are made to be partakers of Christ's divine nature when the marriage is consummated in the Holiest of All, the sacred wedding chamber, on the day of At-One-ment very soon to come!

"Let us be glad and rejoice, and give honour to him: *<u>for the marriage of the Lamb is come</u>, and his wife hath made herself ready.* And to her was granted that she should be arrayed in fine linen, clean and white: for the fine linen is the righteousness of saints" (Rev. 19:7, 8) (emphasis added).

"...The bridegroom came; and they that were ready went in with him to the marriage..." (Matt. 25:10).

God's promise is sure to us, this righteousness of Christ shall be unto us and within us if we will believe the Word of God—even as the children of Israel were to look upon the snake on the pole that Moses lifted up in the wilderness.

Righteousness by faith is to simply and sincerely believe in the promise and provision God has given, and by faith to make it our own through the merits of Jesus Christ!

Look and Live!

"And the LORD answered me, and said, Write the vision, and make it plain upon tables, that he may run that readeth it. *For the vision is yet for an appointed time*, but at the end it shall speak, and not lie: though it tarry, wait for it; because it will surely come, it will not tarry. Behold, his soul which is lifted up is not upright in him: but the just shall live by his faith." — *"The righteousness of God…"* (Hab. 2:2–4; Rom. 3:21, 22) (emphasis added).

"God came from Teman, and the Holy One from mount Paran. Selah. His glory covered the heavens, and the earth was full of his praise. And *his brightness was as the light; he had bright beams coming out of his side: and there was the hiding of his power*" (Hab. 3:3–4, KJV margin) (emphasis added).

"And as Moses lifted up the serpent in the wilderness, even so must the Son of man be lifted up: That whosoever believeth in him should not perish, but have eternal life. For God so loved the world, that he gave his only begotten Son, that whosoever believeth in him should not perish, but have everlasting life. For God sent not his Son into the world to condemn the world; but that the world through him might be saved. He that believeth on him is not condemned: but he that believeth not is condemned already, because he hath not believed in the name of the only begotten Son of God" (John 3:14–18).

"And this is the condemnation, that *light is come into the world,* (also see Hab. 3:4 KJV margin) **and men loved darkness rather than light, because their deeds were evil. For every one that doeth evil hateth the light, neither cometh to the light, lest his deeds should be reproved. But he that doeth truth cometh to the light, that his deeds may be made manifest, that they are wrought in God"** (John 3:19–21) (emphasis added).

In the atonement, the character of God is revealed.

SPECIAL REFERENCE SECTION

[i] (pg. 18) "'I saw a new heaven and a new earth: for the first heaven and the first earth were passed away.' Revelation 21:1. The fire that consumes the wicked purifies the earth. Every trace of the curse is swept away. No eternally burning hell will keep before the ransomed the fearful consequences of sin.

One reminder alone remains: Our Redeemer will ever bear the marks of His crucifixion. Upon His wounded head, upon His side, His hands and feet, are the only traces of the cruel work that sin has wrought. Says the prophet, beholding Christ in His glory: **"He had bright beams coming out of His side: and there was the hiding of His power"** (Hab. 3:4, margin). *That pierced side whence flowed the crimson stream that reconciled man to God—there is the Saviour's glory, there "the hiding of His power."* "Mighty to save," through the sacrifice of redemption, He was therefore strong to execute justice upon them that despised God's mercy. And the tokens of His humiliation are His highest honor; through the eternal ages the wounds of Calvary will show forth His praise and declare His power."

White, Ellen G. *The Great Controversy.* Mountain View, CA: Pacific Press Publishing Association, 1911, p. 674 (emphasis added).

Please get and read this book and believe God's special message therein!

[ii] (pg. 29) **"And he is the propitiation for our sins: and not for ours only, but also for the sins of the whole world"** (1 John 2:2).

And He is the propitiationor And He Himself is a propitiation: there is no article in the Greek. Note the present tense throughout; "We have an Advocate; He is a propitiation." *This condition of things is perpetual; it is not something that took place once and for all a long time ago.* In His glorified body the Son is ever acting thus. Contrast He "laid down His life for us" (1 John 3:16).

Beware of the unsatisfactory explanation that *propitiation* is the abstract for the concrete, *propitiation* (ἱλασμός) for *propitiator* (ἱλαστήρ). Had John written *propitiator* we should have lost half the truth: that our Advocate propitiates by offering Himself. He is both High Priest and Victim, both Propitiator and Propitiation. It is quite obvious that He is the former; the office of Advocate includes it. It is not at all obvious that He is the latter: very rarely does an advocate offer himself as a propitiation.

The word *propitiation* occurs nowhere in New Testament, but here and in 1 John 4:10; in both places without the article and followed by "for our sins." It signifies any action that has expiation as its object. Thus "the ram of the atonement" (Num. 5:8) is "the ram of the propitiation or expiation," where the same Greek word as is used here is used in the LXX.

Compare Ezek. 44:27; Num. 29:11; Lev. 25:9. The LXX. of "there is forgiveness with Thee" (Ps. 130:4) is remarkable: literally rendered it is "before Thee is the propitiation" (ὁ ἱλασμός). So also the Vulgate, apud Te propitiatio est. And this is the idea that we have here: Jesus Christ, as being righteous, is ever present before the Lord as the propitiation. With this we should compare the use of the cognate verb in Hebrews 2:17 and cognate substantive Romans 3:25 and Hebrews 9:5. From these passages it is clear that in New Testament the word is closely connected with that special form of expiation that takes place by means of an offering or sacrifice...for our sins. Literally, concerning (περὶ) our sins: our sins are the matter respecting which the propitiation goes on. Notice that it is "our sins," not "our sin": the sins that we are daily committing, and not merely the sinfulness of our nature, are the subject of the propitiation.

Cambridge Bible Commentary. On 1 John 2:2. London: Cambridge University Press (emphasis added).

[iii] (pg. 47) "Christ was not compelled to endure this cruel treatment. The yoke of obligation was not laid upon Him to undertake the work of redemption. Voluntarily He offered Himself, a willing, spotless sacrifice. He was equal with God, infinite and omnipotent. He was above all finite requirements. He was Himself the law in character. Of the highest angels it could not be said that they had never borne a yoke. The angels all bear the yoke of dependence, the yoke of obedience. They are the appointed messengers of Him who is Commander of all heaven.

No one of the angels could become a substitute and surety for the human race, for their life is God's; they could not surrender it. On Christ alone the human family depended for their existence. *He is the eternal, self-existent Son, on whom no yoke had come.* When God asked, 'Whom shall I send, and who will go for Us?' Christ alone of the angelic host could reply, 'Here am I; send Me.' He alone had covenanted before the foundation of the world to become a surety for man. He could say that which not the highest angel could say— 'I have power over My own life. I have power to lay it down, and I have power to take it again'" (John 10:18).

White, Ellen G. *Manuscript Releases*, Vol. 12, 1990. Silver Spring, MD: Ellen G. White Estate, 1990, p. 395.2 (emphasis added).

[iv] (pg. 51) "It is the spirit that quickeneth; the flesh profiteth nothing: the words that I speak unto you, they are spirit, and they are life" (John 6:57, 63). Christ is not here referring to His doctrine, but to His person, *the divinity of His character*."

White, Ellen G. *Selected Messages*, Book 1. Washington, DC: Review and Herald Publishing Association, 1958, p. 249 (emphasis added).

[v] (pg. 87) "By this transaction (transference of sin to the sanctuary by blood) the altar became defiled, and particularly the horns. For this reason it became necessary to make an atonement upon the altar once a year with the blood of a sin offering. This atonement was accomplished when the priest took the pure blood of the Lord's goat, upon whom no sins had been placed, and put it upon the horns of the altar round about. 'And he shall go out unto the altar that is before Jehovah, and make atonement for it; and shall take the blood of the bullock, and the blood of the goat, and put it upon the horns of the altar round about. And he shall sprinkle of the blood upon

it with his finger seven times, and cleanse it, and hallow it from the uncleannesses of the children of Israel'" (Lev. 16:18, 19, ARV). *As during the year these horns had been polluted by the sin-charged blood that had been placed upon them, so now they are cleansed with sinless blood used on the Day of Atonement.*

It is of interest to note that on the Day of Atonement the atoning blood was placed only on the objects that had previously been defiled. No blood was placed on the laver or the candlestick or the table of show bread, for no blood had previously been applied to them.

But blood was applied to the mercy seat, where the blood of the bullock had been sprinkled.

The altar of incense and the altar of burnt offering were also sprinkled, and blood put on the horns (Exod. 30:10; 16:18, 19), for these altars had previously been defiled in the daily service. Of the veil we have no clear record that any blood was sprinkled on it, either in the daily service or in the cleansing on the Day of Atonement. The Bible statement is that the blood was sprinkled "before" the veil, which is probably the correct reading (Lev. 4:6, 17).

However, once a year the veil was taken down and a new one hung up. We therefore hold that blood both pollutes and cleanses. What the blood does, depends upon the value of the of blood used. The life measures the blood, and the blood the life; for "the life of the flesh is in the blood" (Lev. 17:11).

"If it is a sinful life, the blood pollutes; if it is a sinless life, it cleanses. In harmony with this is the fact that while sin was confessed over the sacrifice in the daily service, *there is no record that sin was confessed over the Lord's goat in the yearly service.*"

Andreasen, M. L. *The Sanctuary Service*. Hagerstown, MD: Review and Herald Publishing Association, pp. 148–149 (emphasis added).

[vi] (pg. 93) "(Lev. 14:4–8 quoted) The wonderful symbol of the living bird dipped in the blood of the bird slain and then set free to its joyous life, is to us the symbol of the atonement. There death and life blended, presenting to the searcher for truth the hidden treasure, the union of the pardoning blood with the resurrection and life of our Redeemer.

The bird slain was over living water; that flowing stream was a symbol of the ever-flowing, ever-cleansing efficacy of the blood of Christ, the Lamb slain from the foundation of the world, the fountain that was open for Judah and Jerusalem, wherein they may wash and be clean from every stain of sin. We are to have free access to the atoning blood of Christ. This we must regard as the most precious privilege, the greatest blessing, ever granted to sinful man. And how little is made of this great gift! How deep, how wide and continuous is this stream! To every soul thirsting after holiness there is repose, there is rest, there is the quickening influence of the Holy Spirit, and then the holy, happy, peaceful walk and precious communion with Christ. Then, oh, then, can we intelligently say with John, 'Behold the Lamb of God, that taketh away the sin of the world."

The Seventh-Day Adventist Bible Commentary: Volume 1: General Articles: Commentary on Genesis, Exodus, Leviticus, Numbers, Deuteronomy. Washington, DC: Review and Herald Publishing Association, p. 1111.

[vii] (pg. 94) "Thank God that He who spilled His blood for us, lives to plead it, lives to make intercession for every soul who receives Him. 'If we confess our sins, he is faithful and just to forgive us our sins, and to cleanse us from all unrighteousness.' The blood of Jesus Christ cleanses us from all sin. It speaketh better things than the blood of Abel, for Christ ever liveth to make intercession for us. We need to keep ever before us the efficacy of the blood of Jesus. That life-cleansing, life-sustaining blood, appropriated by living faith, is our hope. We need to grow in appreciation of its inestimable value, for it speaks for us only as we by faith claim its virtue, keeping the conscience clean and at peace with God.

This is represented as the pardoning blood, inseparably connected with the resurrection and life of our Redeemer, illustrated by the ever-flowing stream that proceeds from the throne of God, the water of the river of life."

The Seventh-Day Adventist Bible Commentary: Volume 7: Philippians to Revelation. Washington, DC: Review and Herald Publishing Association, pp. 947–948 (emphasis added).

AUTHOR'S COMMENTARY

Before we begin, please allow me to say a few things concerning this book and its message. This message is not traditional Adventist theology. Its purpose is to advance and I hope, complete, light and truth God has already given to the Seventh-day Adventist church. There are many examples in our rich history where Ellen G. White, being guided by the Spirit of God, endorsed and sided with views that were not the mainstream view in Adventism. Actually one of the best examples of this is the messages of Righteousness by Faith which were brought to our church by Jones and Waggoner. Several concepts in this book build upon that light Ellen G. White endorsed. Yet those concepts are not as well known in Adventism generally. There are many Adventist ministers who preach that that 1888 light has still not been accepted generally and rather that the views which the denomination held before 1888, which were corrected by the 1888 message and the endorsements of EGW, those old views still form the dominant and orthodox view of the law and the covenants generally taught in our church. In other words, many ministers in good standing and who love our church deeply teach that the disagreements that were brought to a head in 1888 are still present today; and still today as a church we have ministers and ministries teaching these concepts - many according to the old view and others teaching according to the new view brought out in 1888.

I didn't write this book to cover that ground; there have been others, more qualified than me, who have written books about this history and I will reference their works. My desire is to share a message that builds upon that advanced light from 1888, but I believe that some of the difficulty my early readers had is because they are either unaware that I am building upon light already given or perhaps do not agree with the light already given, therefore they cannot see the Adventist foundations in the message that I am sharing which builds upon that light.

So in my explanations of theological concepts that are of concern it will be necessary for me to either teach for the first time or review briefly that 1888 light (obviously while proving this is indeed what was taught by Jones and Waggoner and was endorsed by the Spirit of Prophecy and is not my opinion). I will not take further time to do that now, already you have been gracious to read this introduction… I hope to show those 1888 foundations in the context of the areas of concern; that may be the best way that you could apply the concepts to the topics of concern or at least see why I'm saying what I am saying.

Remember, we don't have to personally agree on these things. This book will give a challenging message regardless of how we word it. But I do hope to show you without fail the background and inspired reasons for each theological concept I have expressed that has been highlighted as of concern. I will also quote the works of other Adventist ministers who have expressed some of these concepts especially well and have helped me in better understanding the message I believe I have been given to share.

Please be prayerful as we undertake this in the sight of God… and lastly please remember these important admonitions from Ellen G. White concerning new messages that she foretold and tried to prepare the church, because they would indeed come:

"There is no excuse for anyone in taking the position that there is no more truth to be revealed, and that all our expositions of Scripture are without an error. The fact that certain doctrines have been held as truth for many years by our people, is not a proof that our ideas are infallible. Age will not make error into truth, and truth can afford to be fair. No true doctrine will lose anything by close investigation." {CW 35.2}

"Some have asked me if I thought there was any more light for the people of God. Our minds have become so narrow that we do not seem to understand that the Lord has a mighty work to do for us. Increasing light is to shine upon us; for "the path of the just is as the shining light, that shineth more and more unto the perfect day."—*The Review and Herald*, June 18, 1889. {CW 34.2}

Also deeply consider the following counsel concerning the 1888 message... It is especially relevant because when God sends new and advanced thoughts to the church they are often perceived as changing the foundations of the faith when that was not the case, just as when Christ came to the Jews:

"There is a bracing of the mind, an opposition of the soul brought to the investigation of the Scriptures. This leaves such souls where Satan can impress them. In Minneapolis God gave precious gems of truth to His people in new settings. This light from heaven by some was rejected with all the stubbornness the Jews manifested in rejecting Christ, and there was much talk about standing by the old landmarks. But there was evidence they knew not what the old landmarks were. There was evidence and there was reasoning from the word that commended itself to the conscience; but the minds of men were fixed, sealed against the entrance of light, because they had decided it was a dangerous error removing the 'old landmarks' when it was not moving a peg of the old landmarks, but they had perverted ideas of what constituted the old landmarks." – {1888 518.1}

Here are some statements from earlier drafts of my book that caused early readers concern. I will attempt to explain my use and meaning of these ideas below:

"Don't let Me fall"

This statement quite possibly can be troubling to certain Adventists in two ways. 1) Persons who believe that Christ's work was finished at the Cross and therefore, there is no conceivable way Christ's mission could in any way fail or come short; 2) Similarly related, persons who believe that it is simply not possible for God to fail or even risk failure. I want to say, in most all these cases we will cover, I do see your concerns as valid, but please humbly allow me to share my evidence concerning all these areas, as to why I wrote what I did.

I'll address the second concern first: if it is possible for God to fail or even risk failure. Hopefully some EGW quotes will help us settle this quickly and move on:

"***Those who claim that it was not possible for Christ to sin, cannot believe that He really took upon Himself human nature***. But was not Christ actually tempted, not only by Satan in the wilderness, but all through His life, from childhood to manhood? In all points He was tempted as we are, and because He successfully resisted temptation under every form, He gave man the perfect example, and through the ample provision Christ has made, we may become partakers of the divine nature, having escaped the corruption which is in the world through lust." {7BC 929.2}

It was possible for Christ to sin, with all the attending unthinkable results. If were not possible for Christ to sin then He could not be our example.

Concerning failure:

"Without the cross they would be no more secure against evil than were the angels before the fall of Satan. **Angelic perfection *failed* in heaven. Human perfection *failed* in Eden,**

the paradise of bliss. All who wish for security in earth or heaven must look to the Lamb of God." {5BC 1132.8}

This point is significant. You may say *but that's angels and perfect humans who failed, not God or Deity…* but this helps to illustrate the main point of the risk God took and is taking for our salvation as we address the first concern now:

How can it be thought of at all that Christ and the government of heaven could fail after Jesus' death on the Cross?

This teaching within Adventism has been given a name and it is called 'Last Generation Theology'. The idea is purely Adventist and is expressed here by EGW in several places in *The Great Controversy*:

"***Those who are living upon the earth when the intercession of Christ shall cease in the sanctuary above are to stand in the sight of a holy God without a mediator***." {GC 425.2}

"When the third angel's message closes, mercy no longer pleads for the guilty inhabitants of the earth. The people of God have accomplished their work. They have received 'the latter rain,' 'the refreshing from the presence of the Lord,' and ***they are prepared for the trying hour before them***… When He leaves the sanctuary, darkness covers the inhabitants of the earth. In that fearful time the righteous must live in the sight of a holy God without an intercessor." {GC 613.2-614.1}

"As Satan influenced Esau to march against Jacob, so he will stir up the wicked to destroy God's people in the time of trouble. And as he accused Jacob, he will urge his accusations against the people of God. He numbers the world as his subjects; but the little company who keep the commandments of God are resisting his supremacy. ***If he could blot them from the earth, his triumph would be complete***… He has an accurate knowledge of the sins which he has tempted them to commit, and he presents these before God in the most exaggerated light, representing this people to be just as deserving as himself of exclusion from the favor of God. He declares that the Lord cannot in justice forgive their sins and yet destroy him and his angels. He claims them as his prey and demands that they be given into his hands to destroy.

"As Satan accuses the people of God on account of their sins, the Lord permits him to try them to the uttermost. ***Their confidence in God, their faith and firmness, will be severely tested.***" {GC 618.2,3}

There is a lot here, but let's see if we can bring out the important points. At the end of time, God is depending on His demonstration of grace manifested in the 144,000 to finally defeat Satan and close the great controversy. Here is where the earlier quotes are helpful to understand how great a demonstration this is. It was possible for even Christ to sin, so we know it is possible for one of the 144,000 to sin. Also both angelic and human perfection failed in the past, so we should not say that there is no risk here. And finally, although Christ defeated Satan at the Cross, The Great Controversy quoted above says that if Satan could destroy the 144,000 "*his triumph would be complete*". Satan could still win the great controversy if he can defeat *Christ* living in the 144,000, who are still on earth in fallen sinful nature (pertaining to their physical human natures), but their moral natures at this time have been "born from above," like unto Christ in His earthly life (see John 3:3 KJV margin). ... Therefore I received a message years ago, expressed in the simple admonition: "Don't let Me fall," which I believe is addressed to God's remnant people, for whom this message is sent.

Here are a few expressions from a beloved Adventist minister on this topic:

The Last Generation

"**THE final demonstration of what the gospel can do in and for humanity is still in the future**. Christ showed the way. He took a human body, and in that body demonstrated the power of God. Men are to follow His example and prove that what God did in Christ, He can do in every human being who submits to Him. The world is awaiting this demonstration. (Romans 8: 19) When it has been accomplished, the end will come. God will have fulfilled His plan. He will have shown Himself true and Satan a liar. His government will stand vindicated…

"Job's case is recorded for a purpose. While we grant its historicity, we believe that it has also a wider meaning. God's people in the last days will pass through an experience similar to Job's. They will be tested as he was; they will have every earthly stay removed; Satan will be given permission to torment them. In addition to this the Spirit of God will be withdrawn from the earth, and the protection of earthly governments removed. God's people will be left alone to battle with the powers of darkness. They will be perplexed, as was Job. But they, as did he, will hold fast their integrity. In the last generation God will stand vindicated. In the remnant Satan will meet his defeat. The charge that the law cannot be kept will be met and fully refuted. God will produce not only one or two who keep His commandments, but a whole group, spoken of as the 144,000. They will reflect the image of God fully. They will have disproved Satan's accusation against the government of heaven…

"God, to make the demonstration complete, does one more thing. He hides Himself. The sanctuary in heaven is closed. The saints cry to God day and night for deliverance, but He appears not to hear. God's chosen ones are passing through Gethsemane. They are having a little taste of Christ's experience those three hours on the cross. Seemingly they must fight their battles alone. They must live in the sight of a holy God without an intercessor… Will they stand the test? To human eyes it seems impossible…

"The matter of greatest importance in the universe is not the salvation of men, important as that may seem. The most important thing is the clearing of God's name from the false accusations made by Satan. The controversy is drawing to a close. God is preparing His people for the last great conflict. Satan is also getting ready. **The issue is before us and will be decided in the lives of God's people.** ***God is depending upon us as He did upon Job.*** **Is His confidence well placed?** It is a wonderful privilege vouchsafed this people to help clear God's name by our testimony." {M.L. Andreasen, *The Sanctuary Service*, chapter 21, "The Last Generation"}

The Atonement was not completed at the Cross...

Now to address the first concern by some believers that the Atonement was finished at the Cross. We Adventists understand that Christ's Atonement was not completed at the Cross (although in some ways orthodox Adventism has shifted on this point):

"(Christ has) ascended on high to be our only mediator in the sanctuary in Heaven, where, *with his own blood* he makes atonement for our sins; ***which atonement so far from being made on the cross***, which was but the offering of the sacrifice, is the very last portion of his work as priest." {1872 Seventh Day Adventist Statement of Beliefs}

And Sister White's very clear statement in *The Great Controversy*, that Christ's atonement was not finished at the Cross, but "began" there, to be "completed" in heaven:

"The intercession of Christ in man's behalf in the sanctuary above is as essential to the plan of salvation as was His death upon the cross. **By His death He *began* that work which after His resurrection He ascended to *complete in heaven*.** We must by faith enter within the veil, "whither the forerunner is for us entered." Hebrews 6:20. There the light from the cross of Calvary is reflected. There we may gain a clearer insight into the mysteries of redemption." {GC 489.1}

I spent an important part of our attention potential on this because this is an important basis for the message of my book. Let us move on now.

"And the Lamb set free"

We may have already demonstrated what is meant by this phrase when we addressed the first concern; but I do want to make a point here about following the Bible and not simply going with church orthodoxy.

Here is an interesting statement in our 27 fundamental beliefs about the sanctuary doctrine:

Chapter 23: Christ's Ministry in the Heavenly Sanctuary

"...But there is more to salvation history. It reaches beyond the cross. Jesus' resurrection and ascension direct our attention to **the heavenly sanctuary, where, no longer the Lamb**, He ministers as priest."

The text from our 27 fundamental beliefs on the heavenly sanctuary says that Jesus ministers "no longer the Lamb"... I respectfully disagree, for in the book of Revelation Jesus is called the Lamb more than any other name, especially here:

"And I beheld, and, lo, in the midst of the throne and of the four beasts, and in the midst of the elders, **stood a Lamb as it had been slain**, having seven horns and seven eyes, which are the seven Spirits of God sent forth into all the earth." {Rev. 5:6}

So He is not only a Lamb, but a Lamb as it hath been slain, and that in the heavenly temple.

The reason for the belief being stated as Jesus no longer being a Lamb is rooted in another doctrinal controversy which we will have to address soon.

Now the idea that we deliver the Lamb is plain, in that Jesus cannot close His sanctuary ministry and return as King of kings until He has a people on earth who fulfill Rev. 14:12: "here is the patience of the saints: here are they that keep the commandments of God and the faith of Jesus." This concept builds largely on the thoughts and teachings brought out while addressing the first concern about "Don't let Me fall."

"The ceremonial portions of God's law have not been abolished"

This is a monumental point and is the foundation for many statements I make in the book. It is also a point that potentially could be controversial, but I hope I can demonstrate to you the evidence for why I make such a statement. But first let me make clear what I mean and what I do not mean…

What I am not saying is that I believe that the earthly expressions of the ceremonial law should be observed or that they have not passed away. What I am saying is that Christ does indeed fulfill the ceremonial law in heaven therefore it cannot be said the law is passed away.

EGW expresses this point and makes the distinction in *The Desire of Ages*:

"'In the midst of the week He shall cause the sacrifice and the oblation to cease.' Dan. 9:27. In the spring of A. D. 31, Christ the true sacrifice was offered on Calvary. Then the veil of the temple was rent in twain, showing that the sacredness and significance of the sacrificial service had departed. **The time had come for the <u>*earthly*</u> sacrifice and oblation to cease.**" {DA 233.2}

It was the earthly expression of the ceremonial law that ceased. Now see that Christ is fulfilling the ceremonial law in heaven:

"As you come with humble heart, you find pardon, for Christ Jesus is represented as continually <u>*standing at the altar, momentarily offering up the sacrifice*</u> for the sins of the world. He is a minister of the true tabernacle which the Lord pitched and not man. The typical shadows of the Jewish tabernacle no longer possess any virtue. A daily and yearly typical atonement is no longer to be made, **<u>but the atoning *sacrifice* through a mediator is essential</u>** because of the constant commission of sin. Jesus is officiating in the presence of God, offering up His shed blood, as it had been a lamb slain. **Jesus presents the**

oblation offered for every offense and every shortcoming of the sinner." {1SM 343.4}

Notice that heavenly "sacrifice and oblation" continue until all is fulfilled.

In heaven Christ is our true High Priest, in the sanctuary, standing at the altar and the mercy seat… all these are things we only know about because God detailed for us the ceremonial law on earth. He gave this so that we can understand to a great extent what Christ is doing for us in heaven, as far as what is important for us to know.

"The Error of Dispensationalism"

Dispensationalism is the dominant, orthodox view in Christianity and also in the Adventist church. But this view of teaching the covenants in the Bible is in fact error, but we did not know this until Jones and Waggoner brought the 1888 message.

I will attempt to demonstrate the background of these things in a basal manner. First, please consider this short quote summing up why this is a necessary component to truly understanding Jones and Waggoner's message:

"E. J. Waggoner's message of righteousness by faith was constructed in connection with his understanding of the law and the two covenants. To misunderstand, discount, or reject any aspect of this trio would be to distort the 1888 message." {Paul Penno, *Calvary at Sinai*, page 71}

Another author quoted this SDA history and teaching this way (bear in mind that in the 1888 disagreement the leadership of G.I. Butler and Uriah Smith were foremost in advocating the 'old view' and opposing the 'new view' being taught by Jones and Waggoner):

"Adventists under the leadership of Uriah Smith, G.I. Butler and others taught a view on the covenants that they felt answered all the objections coming from the Christian world [(here Smith gives an example of one of those objections:)

"Briefly stated, then, their claim is this: That the ten commandments constituted the first or old covenant; that that covenant was faulty and has been done away" (Uriah Smith, *The Two Covenants*, p. 3)] – Smith taught that there was really only one plan, only one covenant that God had made with Abraham which He carried out in two phases, the old and new covenant: "In the accomplishment of that promise which He gave to Abraham there were two stages, *two dispensations*, and by each of these He was carrying on the same idea." {Remarks of Eld. Uriah Smith, Bible School, Feb 19, 1890, pp. 5, 10} (emphasis added)

Most of these explanations had virtually one goal in mind, to convince the Christian world that the old covenant was the ceremonial law—the law to which the Galatians was speaking ("the schoolmaster")—and that the ten commandments were still binding, including the Sabbath.

In contrast, Jones' and Waggoner's understanding of the covenants was not based on opinions acquired in an attempt to defend against false accusations from the Christian world, but rather based on an understanding of the everlasting gospel which permeates the entire Bible. *They saw the two covenants not as representing two dispensations or matters of time, but rather representing the condition of the heart.* (emphasis added) Man can today be just as much under the old covenant as the people were who stood at Mt Sinai…

Waggoner made it clear several times that "in the first covenant the people promised to keep all the commandments of God, so as to be worthy of a place in His kingdom. This was a virtual promise to make themselves righteous." {E. J. Waggoner, "The Promises to Israel: The Covenant of Promise," *Present Truth*, Dec. 10, 1896, p. 789}

"…the everlasting covenant made with Abraham (the same as the "new" or "second" covenant) was not a contract, in the sense of two equal parties making a deal, but the promises of God to Abraham and his response of faith. Abraham believed

God and it was counted him for righteousness. Abraham gave more than a mental assent, he appreciated and treasured in his heart the promises of God and in this sense kept the covenant with God."

(again quoting Waggoner from the same *Present Truth* article quoted above) "At Mt. Sinai the Lord tested them (the children of Israel) again, referring to the covenant long before given to Abraham, and exhorted them to keep it, telling them the sure results. The covenant with Abraham was a covenant of faith and they could keep it simply by keeping the faith. God did not ask them to enter into another covenant with Him, but only to accept His covenant of peace. The proper response of the people therefore would have been: "Amen, even so, O Lord, let it be done unto us according to thy will." Instead the people responded by making a promise themselves: "All that the Lord has spoken we will do" (Exodus 19:8)." {Ron Duffield, "The Return of the Latter Rain," pp. 304–309}

EGW endorsed the 1888 message of the Law in Galatians and the Covenants as taught by Jones and Waggoner:

"Now I tell you here before God, **that the covenant question, as it has been presented, is the truth. It is the light**. In clear lines it has been laid before me. And those that have been resisting the light, I ask you whether they have been working for God, or for the devil. It is the clear light of heaven, and it means much to us. It means to show us that you cannot depend upon your own smartness and your criticisms, but you must hang your helpless soul upon Jesus Christ, and upon Him alone. God help you to see. God help you to understand… I have born testimony after testimony, but it has not had any weight. They have rejected everything but their own ideas. May God help you to not close your hearts and minds to this testimony. May God help you to accept and receive it as truth." {1888 Materials, page 596.2}

"Night before last I was shown that evidences in regard to the covenants were clear and convincing. Yourself (Elder

Uriah Smith), Brother Dan Jones, Brother Porter and others are spending your investigative powers for naught to produce a position on the covenants to vary from the position that Brother Waggoner has presented, When you had received the true light which shineth, you would not have imitated or gone over the same manner of interpretation and misconstruing the Scriptures as did the Jews." {1888 604.2}

"'The law was our schoolmaster to bring us unto Christ, that we might be justified by faith' (Gal. 3:24). **In this scripture, the Holy Spirit through the apostle is speaking especially of the moral law.** The law reveals sin to us, and causes us to feel our need of Christ and to flee unto Him for pardon and peace by exercising repentance toward God and faith toward our Lord Jesus Christ.

"**An unwillingness to yield up preconceived opinions, and to accept this truth, lay at the foundation of a large share of the opposition manifested at Minneapolis against the Lord's message through Brethren {E.J.} Waggoner and {A.T.} Jones.** By exciting that opposition Satan succeeded in shutting away from our people, in a great measure, the special power of the Holy Spirit that God longed to impart to them. The enemy prevented them from obtaining that efficiency which might have been theirs in carrying the truth to the world, as the apostles proclaimed it after the day of Pentecost. *The light that is to lighten the whole earth with its glory was resisted, and by the action of our own brethren has been in a great degree kept away from the world.*" {1SM 234.5,6}

I know that if someone has never studied these subjects before, what I have shared above might not be enough to cause one to understand the importance of what has been revealed nor the conclusions that I have drawn from this… but I will summarize what it means and apply it back to the message of my book:

The 1888 teaching of the covenants maintains that God has only had one way to save humans, both before Christ died on the Cross as well as afterwards, and that is through faith in the atonement of Jesus Christ, His Son. This new covenant is having faith in Messiah like Abel had even in the Old Testament (see Heb. 11:4) and the old covenant is seeking to approach God through external works and disregard of God's commands like Cain; and persons still approach God in one of these two ways today. So the dispensationalist teaching that God had an old covenant in the old testament which was having His people approach Him by works of the ceremonial law and then now in the new testament He now wants people to come to Him by grace through faith of the new covenant is false and incorrect because God always had only one way for His people to approach Him and that was and is always by faith in the Messiah. The old covenant had no salvation, God did not create it and it was based on the promises of the people saying they will do everything God said, thinking they can do what God requires in their own strength (see Exod. 19:7, 8 and Heb. 8:7, 8). Old covenant is being still in unenlightened, spiritual blindness; claiming to worship and serve God but, being prompted by earthly thoughts and carnal motives (which are the basis of character and actions), evincing that the person does not know Him.

That in a nutshell is the 1888 teaching of the covenants. Jones and Waggoner's teaching on the Law in Galatians is simply that in Galatians 3 Paul is talking about the moral law of ten commandments as the law that is "the schoolmaster", whereas prior to that time (and mostly still today) Adventists taught that "the schoolmaster" was the ceremonial law. This is significant because heaven began to show Adventists that our way of interpreting Paul's statements in Galatians 3 (and in similar statements he makes in other epistles), as only referring to the earthly expression of the ceremonial law being done away with, was incorrect.

These teachings are a great paradigm shift in Christian thinking (the Reformation continues) and they remove the hindrances to understanding that God's whole law is still in force. The old view of the covenants was used to do away with the law of God by teaching that now that we are in the times after the Cross, Christians are under grace and the law is done away with. But the 1888, new view of the covenants shows us that the New Covenant was active and was always the only way of salvation, even in the Old Testament times, even when the Jews had the priesthood, the sanctuary and all the ceremonial services. It shows us that the ceremonies that God ordained were not the problem; the performance of these ceremonies were intended to be an expression of their faith in Messiah, in Whom alone they could be accounted righteous. But when the Jews tried to use these rites, which God had indeed ordained, to gain salvation without saving faith in Christ, that became a huge problem and that is what the Bible calls old covenant.

And the 1888 teaching on the law in Galatians causes the Bible student to realize that when Paul says phrases like: **"But after that faith is come, we are no longer under a schoolmaster"** (Gal. 3:25), those expressions are not to be understood as Paul teaching that God's law is abolished, but he is saying that when we are truly converted and receive Jesus in our hearts by the Holy Spirit, we then are no longer trying to serve God with wrong motives and through human efforts unaided by divine power. This is what Paul means in the many ways he tries to communicate this same thought, for example: **"...the letter killeth, but the spirit giveth life"** (2 Cor. 3:6) and **"...to be carnally minded is death, but to be spiritually minded is life and peace"** (Rom. 8:6). And again, **"But even unto this day, when Moses is read, the veil is upon their heart. Nevertheless when it shall turn to the Lord, the veil shall be taken away"** (2 Cor. 3:15, 16). Therefore the 1888 message effectively corrects the two main pillars of error in Bible interpretation (incorrect teaching on what law Paul is speaking about in Galatians 3 and misunderstanding of what is meant by the terms Old and New Covenant) that were/are used to teach that God's law is abolished.

Here is this teaching beautifully expressed by E. J. Waggoner in his book, *The Glad Tidings*:

"Paul says, 'I advanced in the Jews' religion beyond many of mine own age among my countrymen, being more exceedingly zealous for the traditions of my fathers.' It is easy to see that 'the Jews' religion' was not the religion of God and Jesus Christ, but was human tradition. People make a great mistake in considering 'Judaism' as the religion of the Old Testament. The Old Testament no more teaches Judaism than the New Testament teaches Roman Catholicism. **The religion of the Old Testament is the religion of Jesus Christ.** It was His Spirit that was in the prophets, moving them to present **the same Gospel** that the apostles afterwards preached. 1Pet.1:10-12. When Paul was 'in the Jews' religion' he did not believe the Old Testament, which he read and heard read daily, because he did not understand it; if he had, he would have believed on Christ. 'For they that dwell at Jerusalem, and their rulers, because they knew Him not, nor yet the voices of the prophets which are read every Sabbath day, they have fulfilled them in condemning Him.' Acts 13:27." {E.J. Waggoner, *The Glad Tidings*, p. 40, 41} (emphasis added)

I love the way Waggoner expressed his view of the covenants here because it helps us see the beauty in the truth that God has always had only one way to save man. God never desired man to approach Him by works of the law (Judaism) or by disregard of His commands and teachings (Roman Catholicism).

As I have said, the old view of the covenants is more generally taught in Adventism; for example, the book *Ten Commandments Twice Removed* and the Amazing Facts Bible Study – "Written in Stone" teach the covenants according to the old, dispensationalist view. Nevertheless, the new view of the covenants, although it is not the orthodox teaching in Adventism, still it has been taught among us ever since 1888 by some faithful ministers or on occasions here and there… Here is an example in the 3rd quarter Sabbath School lesson of 2017 (which in the introduction acknowledged that it would teach the 1888 message of Jones and Waggoner):

Sabbath afternoon, August 26
Christians who reject the authority of the Old Testament often see the giving of the law on Sinai as inconsistent with the gospel. They conclude that the covenant given on Sinai represents an era, a dispensation, from a time in human history when salvation was based on obedience to the law. But because the people failed to live up to the demands of the law, God (they say) ushered in a new covenant, a covenant of grace through the merits of Jesus Christ. This, then, is their understanding of the two covenants: the old based on law, and the new based on grace.

However common that view may be, it is wrong. Salvation was never by obedience to the law; biblical Judaism, from the start, was always a religion of grace. The legalism that Paul was confronting in Galatia was a perversion, not just of Christianity but of the Old Testament itself. The two covenants are not matters of time; instead they are reflective of human attitudes. They represent two different ways of trying to relate to God, ways that go back to Cain and Abel. The old covenant represents those who, like Cain, mistakenly rely on their own obedience as a means of pleasing God; in contrast, the new covenant represents the experience of those who, like Abel, rely wholly upon God's grace to do all that He has promised.

Wednesday, September 27
"As we have seen all quarter, Paul has basically pitted circumcision against the gospel. **Yet, he's not against the practice itself. Paul has made several strong statements against circumcision (see *Gal. 5:2-4*), but he does not want the Galatians to conclude that being uncircumcised is more pleasing to God than being circumcised**. *That is not his point*,

because one can be just as legalistic about what one does as about what one doesn't do. Spiritually speaking, the issue of circumcision by itself is irrelevant. *True religion is rooted less in external behavior and more in the condition of the human heart.* As Jesus Himself said, a person can look wonderful on the outside but be spiritually rotten on the inside *(Matt. 23:27)*." "The Gospel in Galatians" Sabbath School Lesson, 3rd quarter 2017 (emphasis added)

This is significant because it shows that Paul is not speaking about doing away with God's law, neither moral nor ceremonial in his epistles (starting with Galatians). Paul is speaking about the error of trying to gain salvation by the works of the law and/or offering God a dead formalism... this is old covenant and this is what the problem was (and still is today).

Now, see this expressed clearly by A. T. Jones himself at the General Conference of 1895:

"Christ has set us free from all that in *the second of Colossians, the second of Ephesians, and the third chapter of 2 Corinthians.* Christ has set us free from *formalism and ceremonialism*, from going by rules and resolutions and all these things, but to ever to be guided, actuated, and inspired by the living principle of the life of Jesus Christ itself. The difference between a principle and a rule is that the principle has in it the very life of Christ itself; while the rule is a form that a man makes in which he will express his idea of the principle, and which he would fasten not only upon himself but upon everyone, and make them do just like himself. That is the difference between Christianity and cermonialism. This is the difference between principle and rule. The one is life and freedom; the other is bondage and death…

"We will come at that in another way. What was the cause of all this? What was the cause of that separation between Jews and Gentiles? What was the cause of having a form of godliness without the power? What was the matter with the disciples with Jesus at Samaria? "Enmity" – enmity, sin, self.

But enmity, sin, self, is all self. It was the putting of self in the place of God that not only perverted God's appointed services and forms of service, but added to these a whole mountain of ceremonies and additions of their own, as we have read. What was the object of it all? What were they doing all this for? To be saved, to be righteous. But there is no form or ceremony that even God Himself appointed that can save a man. That is where they missed it. That is where thousands of people still miss it. **And that is the "form of godliness without the power," and that is ceremonialism. And if you will receive it, that is the ceremonial law, that was abolished** by the abolishing in His flesh of the enmity, and so breaking down the middle wall of partition…

"Now, you can see that there is a great deal more in that system of ceremonialism than simply a little passing thing that disturbed the Jews a little while, and then vanished. For, human nature is still, and ever, bothered with it as certainly as the devil lives, as certainly as the enmity is in the human heart. That mind, which "is not subject to the law of God, neither indeed can be," just as certainly as that is in the world, and as long as it is in the world, just so long, the world will be cursed with ceremonialism. And as long as there is any of that in my heart, I shall be in danger of being cursed with ceremonialism." {Eld. Alonzo T. Jones, The 1895 General Conference Bulletin, sermons 25 and 26 The Third Angel's Message} (emphasis added)

Now I'm ready to make my big foundational point which I have spent some time teaching the true principles for and showing some of the evidences: The Law of God, including the ceremonial law is not abolished. The earthly expressions of the ceremonial law have indeed passed away, but not the law itself because Christ is fulfilling the ceremonial law in heaven even now. See this in the following Bible verse:

"And almost all things are **by the law** purged with blood; and without shedding of blood is no remission. **It was therefore**

necessary that the patterns of things in the heavens should be purified with these; but the heavenly things themselves with better sacrifices than these." {Heb. 9:22, 23} (emphasis added)

Paul is teaching that the heavenly sanctuary must be cleansed with "better sacrifices"... Why? Why did he say "it was therefore necessary"? Because in the previous verse he said because it was demanded "by the law", in this case the ceremonial law of course, requires the sanctuary to be cleansed (purged) "with blood". This law Christ is fulfilling in heaven... and it is very important to know that He is fulfilling the law in performing His sanctuary ministry for us:

"For verily I say unto you, Till heaven and earth pass, one jot or one tittle shall in no wise pass from the law, till all be fulfilled." {Matt. 5:18}

"The Lamb of God still sheds His sacred blood"

Now we have come to probably for most people the most challenging thing that I bring out in this book and message. I spent considerable time sharing the foundations, which in themselves had drawn concern, because they support what I am saying here. But the problem is most people don't have those foundations so there is no framework to see any possibility in such a statement. And yet, even for most SDAs who know of the things I have tried to share, even for them such a thought and teaching is still repugnant and un-biblical. Even if you understood and received the foundations I have shared already, such a thought may still seem too far to bridge to... but is it really? Now I must trust that you have read and prayerfully understood what has already been shared. I cannot be so tedious to repeat that again to apply it here. As I said at the start I didn't write this book to cover that ground. We did so here to provide my readers reasons and evidence as to where I am finding biblical ground to say the things I have written... but again is such a teaching too far to bridge? Must one spend so much time in deep study and reviewing all this history and books by many authors to understand this? I say no, it is not necessary…

Nevertheless here a few EGW quotes:

"Children of the Lord, how precious is the promise! How full the atonement of the Saviour for our guilt! The Redeemer, with a heart of unalterable love, ***still sheds his sacred blood*** in the sinner's behalf." {RH, January 9, 1883 par. 21} (emphasis added)

"Still bearing humanity, he ascended to heaven, triumphant and victorious. **He has taken the blood of his atonement into the holiest of all, sprinkled it upon the mercy-seat** and his own garments, and blessed the people. *Soon he will appear the second time to declare that there is no more sacrifice for sin.*" {YI, July 25, 1901 par. 4} (emphasis added)

"The smitten rock was a figure of Christ, and through this symbol the most precious spiritual truths are taught. As the life-giving waters flowed from the smitten rock, so from Christ, "smitten of God," "wounded for our transgressions," "bruised for our iniquities" (Isaiah 53:4, 5), the stream of salvation flows for a lost race. As the rock had been once smitten, so Christ was to be "once offered to bear the sins of many." Hebrews 9:28. Our Saviour was not to be sacrificed a second time; and it is only necessary for those who seek the blessings of His grace to ask in the name of Jesus, pouring forth the heart's desire in penitential prayer. Such prayer will bring before the Lord of hosts the wounds of Jesus, ***and then will flow forth afresh the life-giving blood***, symbolized by the flowing of the living water for Israel." {PP 411.3} (emphasis added)

"Christ as high priest within the veil ***so immortalized Calvary*** that though He liveth unto God, ***He dies continually*** to sin, and thus if any man sin, he has an advocate with the Father." {1SM 343.1} (emphasis added)

"Christ is our Mediator and officiating High Priest in the presence of the Father. He was shown to John as a Lamb that had been slain, ***as in the very act of pouring out His blood***

in the sinner's behalf. When the law of God is set before the sinner, showing him the depth of his sins, he should then be pointed to the Lamb of God, that taketh away the sin of the world. He should be taught repentance toward God and faith toward our Lord Jesus Christ. Thus will the labor of Christ's representative be in harmony with His work in the heavenly sanctuary." {4T 395.2} (emphasis added)

I know most will not agree with my taking these in a more literal sense… But let me ask you this quite simply. Is Jesus fulfilling the law of God, even the ceremonial law in heaven? This question is so simple a child can deal with this subject. *If there is a sanctuary in heaven with two apartments as we teach and real furniture and a real ark of the covenant with a mercy-seat upon it… I ask you, will Jesus sprinkle His blood upon it, in fulfillment of His law or not? The question is really that simple.* There are many reasons and foundational teachings that show me unequivocally that He will… but those are not necessary. There were hundreds of prophecies that Jesus fulfilled when He was upon the earth. So many reasons the Pharisees should have believed on Him, but was knowing all these prophecies necessary for the children and the others who believed on Jesus? No, they simply believed He was the Messiah, the Sent of God, based on the plain evidences that were right in front of them, yet that same evidence could not overcome the wrong teachings and wrong understandings in the minds of most of the Jews at the time of Christ.

I am no messiah, nor make any claim to be a prophet, but this message is about Jesus. Again, will Jesus sprinkle His blood upon the mercy-seat in heaven to conclude the services of the Day of Atonement in fulfillment of the law? Everyone can make that decision when the message comes to them… but the focus is more about the why… Why does Jesus do this? Why does He send such a message?

It is to awaken us to the startling reality that actually it is our sins that are fearsome and revolting and treacherous.

And that Christ is looking for, and I say it reverently, needing a remnant of His people to believe the everlasting gospel so that He may cleanse them of sin and He may be "delivered" from His ministration as a Lamb as it hath been slain and High Priest in the heavenly sanctuary:

God says: "Behold, **I am pressed under you, as a cart is pressed that is full of sheaves**." {Amos 2:13}

God says: "**but thou hast made me to serve with thy sins, thou hast wearied me with thine iniquities**." {Isa. 43:24}

"God says, 'Neither will I be with you any more, unless you **awake, and vindicate your Redeemer**.'" {*Selected Messages Book One*, p. 196} (emphasis added)

There is so much more I could say, but that is why I wrote the book!

The topic concerning Jesus' blood, which we just covered, is the basis of very many of the highlighted concerns, just worded differently in several other places.

"The Sacrifice Continues"

Certainly at this point you can see why I understand this to be true. To summarize the reasons that have been shared so far: 1) Christ's atonement was not finished at the Cross, but His atonement continues in the heavenly sanctuary; 2) Christ is still fulfilling the ceremonial law in heaven, which law teaches "without shedding of blood there is no remission: and 3) the law of God teaches us that at the conclusion of the Day of Atonement, the blood of a special sacrifice made *on (during) the Day of Atonement* must be sprinkled on the mercy-seat.

But I want to tarry here briefly and share a witness from a Bible commentary that is not SDA, but by the Bible alone the writer could discern the truth and was brave enough to declare that Jesus' sacrifice continues:

And ***he is the propitiation for our sins***: and not for ours only, but also for *the sins of* the whole world. 1 John 2:2

"**2**. *And He is the propitiation*] Or, *And He* **Himself** *is* **a** *propitiation*: there is no article in the Greek. Note the present tense throughout; 'we *have* an Advocate, He *is* a propitiation': **this condition of things is perpetual, it is not something which took place once for all long ago.** In His glorified Body the Son is ever acting thus. Contrast 'He laid down His life for us' (1 John 3:16). Beware of the unsatisfactory explanation that 'propitiation' is the abstract for the concrete, 'propitiation' (ἱλασμός) for 'propitiator' (ἱλαστήρ). Had S. John written 'propitiator' we should have lost half the truth; viz. **that our Advocate propitiates by offering *Himself*. He is both High Priest and Victim, both Propitiator and Propitiation.** It is quite obvious that He is the former; the office of Advocate includes it. It is not at all obvious that He is the latter: very rarely does an advocate offer himself as a propitiation." **Cambridge Bible for Schools and Colleges** comment on 1 John 2:2 (emphasis added)

But this is the same truth EGW taught:

"The incarnate I AM is **our abiding Sacrifice**. The I AM is our Redeemer, our Substitute, our Surety. He is the Daysman between God and the human soul, our Advocate in the courts of heaven, our unwearying Intercessor, pleading in our behalf His merits and His atoning sacrifice." {ST, May 3, 1899 par. 15} (emphasis added)

"The infinite sufficiency of Christ is demonstrated by His bearing the sins of the whole world. **He occupies the double position of *offerer and of offering, of priest and of victim*.**" (Letter 192, 1906). {7BC 933.7} (emphasis added)

And to show that Christ's work bearing sins is taking place now, even in heaven:

"The priests were commanded to eat in the tabernacle of certain portions of the peace-offering. By partaking of the sacrifice, and bearing their sins before God, **they represented the work that Christ would do for us** *in the heavenly sanctuary, by bearing our sins in his own body*." {ST, April 6, 1888 par. 8} (emphasis added)

Christ's sacrifice continues. It is important we know that. It will help us to accept the work God has for us and the position we must fulfill in these last days by His grace:

"The subject of the sanctuary and the investigative judgment should be clearly understood by the people of God. **All need a knowledge *for themselves* of the position and work of their great High Priest**. *Otherwise it will be impossible for them to exercise the faith which is essential at this time or to occupy the position which God designs them to fill*." {*The Great Controversy*, p. 488.2} (emphasis added)

"The blood of sprinkling which is in heaven" and "the blood of Jesus… is just as literally present in heaven…"

What I am stating here is simply what the scripture, which I quoted in the book, says:

"And to Jesus the mediator of the new covenant, and to the blood of sprinkling, that speaketh better things than that of Abel." {Heb. 12:24}

Once, many years ago, I shared this message with an Adventist pastor at the church I was attending and he answered me by simply saying, that he really didn't continue the study once he saw what I was saying... but what he said he did was search the internet to see if anyone else was teaching what I was expressing and he said he found that no one had come to any similar conclusions, so he didn't think it was worthy of further study because of this. That really concerned me and was another time in my life where I struggled to keep on believing what I felt like God was showing me. So I prayed with tears, 'Lord, how could it be that no one else has seen this?' Afterwards I searched and found this wonderful sermon by none other than the so-called 'prince of preachers', the British Baptist minister Charles Spurgeon – The Blood of Sprinkling… Not having the benefit of the Adventist sanctuary doctrine, this man was able to so wonderfully declare based solely on the Bible testimony:

"Have you not come a long way? Are you not admitted into the very center of the whole revelation? Not yet. A step further lands you where stands your Savior, the Mediator, with the new covenant. Now is your joy complete; but you have a further object to behold. What is in that innermost shrine? What is that which is hidden away in the holy of holies? What is that which is the most precious and costly thing of all, the last, the ultimatum, God's grandest revelation? The precious blood of Christ, as of a lamb without blemish and without spot—the blood of sprinkling. This comes last; it is the innermost truth of the dispensation of grace under which we live. Brethren, when we climb to heaven itself, and pass the gate of pearl, and wend our way through the innumerable hosts of angels, and come even to the throne of God, and see the spirits of the just made perfect, and hear their holy hymn, we shall not have gone beyond the influence of the blood of sprinkling; nay, we shall see it there more truly present than in any other place beside. **"What!" say you, "the blood of Jesus in heaven?" *Yes*.** The earthly sanctuary, we are told, was purified with the blood of bulls and of goats, "but the heavenly things themselves with better sacrifices than these."(Hebrews 9:23) When Jesus entered once for all into the holy place, he entered by his own blood, having obtained eternal redemption for us: **so saith the apostle in the ninth chapter of this epistle**. Let those who talk lightly of the precious blood correct their view ere they be guilty of blasphemy; for the revelation of God knows no lower deep, this is the heart and center of all. The manifestation of Jesus under the gospel is not only the revelation of the Mediator, but especially of his sacrifice. The appearance of God the Judge of all, the vision of hosts of angels and perfect spirits, do but lead up to that sacrifice which is the source and focus of all true fellowship between God and his creatures. This is the character which Jesus wears in the innermost shrine where he reveals himself most clearly to those who are nearest to him. He looks like a lamb that has been slain. There is no sight of him which is more full, more glorious, more complete, than the vision of him as the great sacrifice for sin. The atonement of Jesus is the concentration of the divine glory; all other revelations of God are completed and intensified here. You have not come to the central sun of the great spiritual system of grace till you have come to the blood of sprinkling—to those sufferings of Messiah which are not for himself, but are intended to bear upon others, even as drops when they are sprinkled exert their influence where they fall. Unless you have learned to rejoice in that blood which taketh away sin, you have not yet caught the key-note of the gospel dispensation. The blood of Christ is the life of the gospel. Apart from atonement you may know the skin, the rind, the husk of the gospel; but its inner kernel you have not discovered." A Sermon (No. 1888) Delivered on Lord's-day Morning, February 28th, 1886, by C. H. SPURGEON, At the Metropolitan Tabernacle, Newington - https://archive.spurgeon.org/sermons/1888.php (emphasis added)

"The very soul of the life of Christ," "His Soul, His Life"

In these expressions I am speaking about the Holy Spirit, but I am actually quoting Sister White. Please consider this beautiful passage:

"Christ declared that after his ascension, he would send to his church, as his crowning gift, the Comforter, who was to take his place. This Comforter is the Holy Spirit, —***the soul of his life***, the efficacy of his church, the light and life of the world. With his Spirit Christ sends a reconciling influence and a power that takes away sin." {RH, May 19, 1904 par. 1} (emphasis added)

"The Holy Spirit is the Spirit life-blood (as it were) of the pre-incarnate Christ when He was in 'the form of God': The Soul of His Life"

What I am saying here is drawn from the very important teaching that the Holy Spirit is Christ's Own Spirit, read this carefully:

"Cumbered with humanity, Christ could not be in every place personally; therefore it was altogether for their advantage that He should leave them, go to His father, and send the Holy Spirit to be His successor on earth. ***The Holy Spirit is Himself*** divested of the personality of humanity and independent thereof. He would represent Himself as present in all places by His Holy Spirit, as the Omnipresent." {14MR 23.3} (emphasis added)

The Holy Spirit is the Spirit of Christ, divested or separated from Christ's assumed humanity and is sent to us as His crowning Gift, inseparably connected to His great and eternal sacrifice.

These are the two great teachings of the message of the book. Christ's literal blood in heaven to cleanse the heavenly sanctuary and Christ's Spirit sent into our hearts to cleanse us, who are called in scripture, "the temple(s) of the living God" (2Cor. 6:16)! I believe these two great truths (see Zech. 4:7, last part) are the very means by which the finishing work of Christ will be accomplished, as described by EGW in this short statement:

"There must be a purifying of the soul here upon the earth, in harmony with Christ's cleansing of the sanctuary in heaven." {1888 Materials, p. 27.1}

"Because the closing of the Great Controversy between Christ and Satan involves how Christ's professed followers 'judge' our Lord Jesus and the character of the living God" and "the final cleansing of the sanctuary and judging His people also, in many respects represents that "the time of the judgment of Him has come" (referencing Rev. 14:7)

This was addressed somewhat in the descriptions of Last Generation theology wherein I quoted certain authors at the beginning of this document. Let's consider that God has indeed submitted Himself to be 'judged' (as a manner of expressing this concept) by His created beings… Notice how perfectly what is being expressed in the Psalms and quoted by Paul in Romans shows the issues of the closing of the Great Controversy (which is the context I used the concept):

"As it is written, That thou mightest be justified in thy sayings, **and mightest overcome when thou art** ***judged***." {Rom. 3:4} (emphasis added)

Also here:

"'**Present your case**,' says the LORD. '***Submit your arguments***,' says the King of Jacob." {Isa. 41:21 (NIV)} (emphasis added)

And again:

"**Yet your people say, '*The way of the Lord is not just.*'** But it is their way that is not just." {Ezek. 33:17 (ESV)} (emphasis added)

And here an Adventist pastor (MA from Andrews) explains both how the Greek of Rev 14:7 can be rendered "The hour of the judgment of Him has come" and a little more of the background concerning how the Great Controversy involves God's creation judging Him and His ways:

"And I saw another angel fly in the midst of heaven, having the everlasting gospel to preach unto them that dwell on the earth ..., saying with a loud voice, Fear God and give glory to Him; for the hour of His judgment is come.

Literally, the last clause reads— "Because came the hour of the judgment of Him." The Greek word for "is come" is ηλθεν, a second aorist (past tense) indicative, and can be translated by either the simple English past tense, or in this case by the perfect tense as is done in the KJV. However, how is the phrase, "the judgment of Him," to be understood? It could indicate a simple possessive sense— "His judgment" —or it could mean that God goes on trial, that He faces a judgment— "the judgment of Him" (τηζ κρισεωζ αυτου). The book of Revelation gives a picture of both concepts. In Chapter 20, John sees the "great white throne" and before this throne of God, stand the "dead," and they are "judged" by "those things which were written in the books, according to their works" (vs. 11–12). This is God in judgment— "His judgment." In Chapter 12, after the symbolic representation of a war between "the dragon" and "Michael," a loud voice is heard saying in heaven— "Now is come ... the kingdom of our God and the power of His Christ (Messiah)" (ver. 10). Has the kingdom of God, thus God, been in question?

The question follows— Did the sin problem place God on trial? If answered in the affirmative, then Revelation 14:7 could mean as it literally reads— "the judgment of Him."

—William H. Grotheer, Final Atonement I (https://1ref.us/22c)

...Thus far concludes the author's explanations and reasons for why I have written certain statements that caused concern.

Thank you for prayerfully considering these things ~ Brent

"FOR WE THROUGH THE SPIRIT WAIT FOR THE HOPE OF RIGHTEOUSNESS BY FAITH."

GAL. 5:5

TEACH Services, Inc.
PUBLISHING

www.ingramcontent.com/pod-product-compliance
Lightning Source LLC
Chambersburg PA
CBHW071216160426
43196CB00012B/2326

* 9 7 8 1 4 7 9 6 1 5 0 4 9 *